TRAVELLING HOPEFULLY

TRAVELLING HOPEFULLY

✴ A SPIRITUAL PILGRIMAGE ✴

Robert Fyall

First published 1996
SPCK
Holy Trinity Church
Marylebone Road
London
NW1 4DU

Acknowledgement
Biblical quotations are from the *New International Version*
© 1973, 1978, 1984 by the International Bible Society.
Published by Hodder & Stoughton.

British Library Cataloguing in Publication Data

A catalogue record for this book is available from the
British Library.

ISBN 0-281-04942-4

Typeset by Wilmaset Ltd, Birkenhead, Wirral
Printed in Great Britain by
Biddles Ltd, Guildford and King's Lynn

To Thelma,
my wife and best friend

Contents

Preface

This book is the result of a series of lectures given in Durham Cathedral during their Lent Course in 1995. It was a real honour for a Scottish Presbyterian to lead the course in that great building which a distinguished Scottish Episcopalian described as 'half church of God, half castle 'gainst the Scot'. I am very grateful to the Dean and Chapter for the invitation. Especially my thanks go to Margaret Parker for arranging the course and chairing the meetings with warmth and courtesy.

My grateful thanks also to SPCK for agreeing to publish this and especially to Rachel Boulding, Senior Editor for her interest and kindness. The book has benefited enormously from her many shrewd suggestions and constructive criticisms.

The original lectures were written during a busy time of college and church work, and many people, sometimes unwittingly, have contributed to the thinking behind it. Thanks to David Day, Principal of St John's College for his interest and encouragement in all my writing projects. Those who attended the lectures contributed enormously by their interest, comments and questions and have helped to shape the final form of the book. Chapters 2 to 6 are a somewhat expanded form of the lectures and Chapter 1 a more sustained reflection on the theme of pilgrimage. Some day I must become computer literate. But in the meantime, my grateful thanks to Marianne Young of St John's College, Secretarial Staff. As always, she has gone well beyond the call of duty with good humour and efficiency.

But most of all my grateful thanks to my family who in a very real sense 'lived' with both the lectures and the book. My children Carmen and Drummond prevented me from ever imagining that pilgrimage could be undertaken anywhere but in the real world. My wife Thelma, the companion of my pilgrimage, was the main support and encouragement which made this book possible and it is dedicated to her with love.

Bob Fyall

ONE

Looking for a city:
going on pilgrimage

2 Corinthians 1.10

He has delivered us from such a deadly peril,
and he will deliver us. On him we have set
our hope that he will continue to deliver us.

It was R. L. Stevenson who said that 'to travel
hopefully is a better thing than to arrive'.[1] These
words express memorably the mingled fascination
and frustration of pilgrimage. The very language
we use about life expresses this sense of travelling. We speak of 'milestones', 'turning another
corner', 'we have moved on', 'the next stage'.
The fact that these and many similar phrases have
become clichés and are hardly noticed to be
metaphors show how deeply the pilgrimage idea
has entered our bloodstream. It is part of us and
we cannot avoid it.

Yet it is this very excitement at the thought of
pilgrimage which sometimes makes us uneasy
about the destination. If we are made to travel,
will not the arrival inevitably be an anticlimax?
We shall therefore explore the destination as well
as the journey both in this chapter and particularly
in our final one. What we shall see is that the
arrival is itself a continuing pilgrimage into ever
new discoveries of the immeasurable love of God.[2]

What this book will explore is the theme of pilgrimage as it surfaces over and over again throughout Scripture. In the ancient church Lent was especially a time when instruction in the Bible was given to candidates preparing for baptism. We shall look at the archetypal pilgrim Abraham and his bold leap of faith. Then we shall open a window into the desert pilgrimage of the ancient Israelite community as it journeyed to the promised land. Some of the psalms, the pilgrim songs of God's ancient people, will show us how in their worship they expressed their hopes and fears as they travelled. The focus will then move to an even more climactic event in salvation history as Mary goes on pilgrimage carrying the Word across the Judaean highlands. We shall finish by looking at Jesus 'the author and finisher of our faith', the supreme pilgrim and also the goal of pilgrimage who brings together 'travelling hopefully' and arriving.

This is not a book about physically going on pilgrimage although this will be discussed throughout. Rather it is a book about spiritual pilgrimage, the life of faith seen as a journey. It is about the dynamic and progressive nature of salvation. Naturally I have been helped by many books which reflect on this theme and some of these will be referred to. Two books, however, particularly deserve mention at this point. These are: the anonymous *The Way of the a Pilgrim*[3] and *The Road to Canterbury*[4] by Shirley Du Boulay. These books are from very different traditions and they describe physical pilgrimages but equally important are the way these mirror the inner pilgrimages.

The Way of a Pilgrim describes the wanderings of an anonymous pilgrim of the middle of the nineteenth century who wandered across Russia devoting himself to interior prayer. The story has an artless charm which captivates the reader. The places, people and experiences are all vividly sketched. Yet what is most fascinating is the inner pilgrimage whose story the reader follows with breathless anticipation. It is ultimately this rather than the pilgrim's literal journeys that the book is about.

The Road to Canterbury tells how the author with three companions set out to follow the footsteps of medieval pilgrims from Winchester to St Thomas Becket's shrine at Canterbury. The result is a fascinating evocation of the countryside seen in depth and with a wealth of imaginative insight. The story is worth reading simply for that, but it is also a profound reflection on the spirituality of pilgrimage and the inner journey.

Both these books also exemplify an important principle which has controlled my explanation of biblical passages throughout this book. In exploring the biblical theme of pilgrimage I have considered many people, events, places and ideas. These have been tangible and actual and yet I have seen them with an extra dimension of depth. Thus Abraham is an actual figure and the Negev through which he travelled an actual place.

3

Yet they are also profoundly symbolic; they represent the people and places of pilgrimage.

But the pilgrimage metaphor can be abused. The Bible uses a great number of images to refer to the life of faith: a battle, a feast, a city, a cultivated field and many others. All have their strengths and weaknesses; that is why there is no one picture which covers the whole truth. We need to take them together and allow each to balance the other. We abuse the pilgrimage idea when we make it deny that there is such a thing as truth. Of course, our knowledge is incomplete – 'we know in part' (1 Corinthians 13.12) – and we must have a proper sense of mystery before God and the issues of life and death. Being on pilgrimage means we do not yet 'know as we are known'. But because we cannot know everything we must not go to the extreme of a false modesty which claims that we cannot know anything. Indeed pilgrimage is simply not possible unless we know and are persuaded of certain things. It is possible only if our story is part of God's own story and caught up in his loving purposes.

What are these certainties? The first certainty is that there is a God who is the Creator and that we are part of his purposes. This is clearly stated in that great pilgrimage chapter Hebrews 11, of which verse 6 states: 'And without faith it is impossible to please God, because anyone who comes to him must believe that he exists and that he rewards those who earnestly seek him'. This verse also makes plain the kind of knowledge and certainty we are speaking about. This is not scientific knowledge which can be demonstrated. This is the risky knowledge of relationship, and no relationship is real unless it develops. So right at the beginning, the call to pilgrimage is a call to relationship. It is a call to the journey of faith, to travelling hopefully; a call to be like that great pilgrim Moses who 'persevered because he saw him who is invisible' (Hebrews 11.27).

Sometimes that call will be dramatic, as with Saul of Tarsus on the road to Damascus, or the young playboy who became St Augustine.[5] For many of us it will come in a gentler but no less insistent way. Perhaps our reading will seem to be mysteriously guided, and a voice which we finally recognize to be God's will be drawing us on. Perhaps we will meet people whose lives and words challenge us to commitment. Perhaps circumstances, not of our choosing, will set us on the pilgrim road. So to be a pilgrim means a conviction that God has called us.

This must be linked with a conviction that God continues to guide, that there are resources for pilgrimage. This is the area where this book hopes to make a tiny contribution with its emphasis on drawing from the wells of Scripture and learning from pilgrims of all generations and traditions. There will be a mixture of high romance and humdrum routine. For example, we must not read the story of Abraham as one of high adventure and forget the little connecting phrases such as 'some time after this' and 'much later'. These remind us that the great triumphs of faith were usually followed by long periods of monotonous routine when it would be difficult to keep on going.

It is certain that God will bring us safely to the goal of the journey which Hebrews 11 calls 'the city with foundations whose architect and builder is God'. This we shall also explore in the pages that follow. What is important to note here is that as we travel hopefully from time to time there are experiences that point beyond themselves. Think of our favourite places; not simply that we enjoy being there but that they have a quality which points beyond them and which makes them windows to some greater and deeper reality. Why does certain music tear at our hearts and fill our eyes with tears? Why do some books have an extra quality which make them far more than just 'a good read' and arouse inexpressible emotions? Why can certain sights, sounds, even smells arouse deep emotions of yearning? Above all, what happens when we fall in love and believe that to be eternal? Are these accidents of our chemical and physical make-ups or are they rather the sense that we belong to some fuller and more enduring life?

I believe the reason why these certainties are so vital for pilgrimage is that they reflect that great Story, the story of God himself. The world of time and space in which we live and through which we travel is the creation of God who works continually through it to bring his people to glory and indeed to redeem and renew the whole of his handiwork. Thus our initial call is of a piece with his creation of the first humans. It is significant that the pilgrimage idea already occurs in Genesis 3.8: '...The Lord God as he was walking in the garden in the cool of the day...'[6] Our life of pilgrimage thereafter is part of God's providential control of history. Through failure after failure, God's purpose works undeflected until 'a second Adam to the fight and to the rescue came'. Finally, in the renewal of all things, the book of Revelation 22.3 states 'his servants, will serve him'. The consummation itself will continue a glorious journey of discovery.

So our pilgrimage is continuous — a principle established in the passage from 2 Corinthians which heads this chapter: 'He has delivered us from such a deadly peril, and he will deliver us. On him we have set our hope that he will continue to deliver us'. This has sometimes been called 'the three tenses of salvation' and it illustrates the value of the pilgrimage metaphor of the life of faith. We have not yet arrived and call, journey and destination all belong to God. This is the most vital thing to realize as we go on pilgrimage; it is God who is in charge. Yet this can easily lead to complacency and laziness, though it need not as we consider each of the three phases.

The word translated 'deliver' is a very rich and full one and is used, for example, in the Lord's Prayer — 'Deliver us from evil'. Its Old Testament equivalent particularly refers to the rescue of the Israelites from Egypt. It occurs throughout the

Psalter as a characteristic activity of God for which the psalmists praise him. It is this sense of being delivered that lies at the heart of pilgrimage and causes us to strike out into the unknown.

The sense of having been delivered provides the strongest possible motive for pilgrimage: gratitude. Calls to discipline and self-denial are part of the journey and we shall come to these. Far more important is the sense of gratitude and love which give the impetus which can transform grim struggling into joyful obedience. Gratitude prevents us on the one hand stumbling through the steamy marshlands of self-indulgence and on the other hand trying to walk along a narrow tight rope of legalistic regulations. Gratitude brings us into another sphere altogether, another dimension where obedience is given lovingly and as a response to being forgiven.

This is why the great classics of pilgrimage are all essentially joyful texts. They contain stern problems and costly disciplines but ultimately they shine with the light of love. One of the great psalms of pilgrimage says: 'My soul yearns, even faints for the courts of the Lord; my heart and my flesh cry out for the living God' (Psalm 84.2). This psalm is not blind to the hazards and struggles of pilgrimage but this is swallowed up in the sense of gratitude to God. Continual gratitude for what God has done is the great blessing of looking back to our call to pilgrimage.

We will not, however, travel very far if we try to dwell in the past and draw all our nourishment from a first experience of God's grace. Our text also says 'he will deliver us', which has the sense of continual deliverance. At one time it was common in some Christian circles for people to give testimonies. Many of these were moving, sometimes dramatic and usually very sincere. The trouble was that many simply concentrated on the initial call of God which may have been many years ago and said little or nothing on the present and continuing experience of God's grace. A man, once famed for his moving testimony, became known as the years passed for repeating the same thing word for word from yellowing dog-eared notes. On one occasion he was frantically searching in an old dresser where he kept these notes before going out to speak yet again. Eventually in dismay he shouted to his wife: 'The mice have eaten my testimony!' It is all too easy for the mice to eat our testimony unless our experience of God is continually renewed.

This is where the daily and hourly experience of God's deliverance is so vital. The experience of pilgrimage in the present is one of people who have not yet arrived. There has often been a tendency, already evident in New Testament times to claim for the Church on earth what is only true of the Church in heaven. The fact that the kingdom has now come in Christ is often taken to mean that we can on the journey experience all that belongs to the 'not yet' of the arrival. This apparently was happening in the Church at Corinth and may lie behind the opening verse of the famous chapter 13 of 1 Corinthians: 'If I speak in the tongues of humans and of angels, but have not love, I am only a resounding gong or a clanging cymbal'. It may be that there were those who were already claiming to speak in 'the tongues of angels', that is the language of heaven and speaking as if they had already arrived and no longer needed the desert disciplines of pilgrimage.

These disciplines, as we shall see, are both personal and communal and involve especially allowing the Bible to become part of our bloodstream and being open to the voice of God in daily prayer. These are the common wells for pilgrims across the earth and across the centuries. But as we travel together we will try to learn from our pilgrim companions. And surely there can never have been a time when so many resources, both reprints of the classics and new works, have been available to help us as we journey. Some remarks can be usefully made about this wealth of material available to us.

The first is that we shall draw deeply from different wells, not necessarily consuming all we find but open to find refreshment where we can. Some will find strength in the limpid clarity and sense of God's presence in creation in Celtic spirituality. Some will be moved by the tender and poignant meditations on our Lord's sufferings by Julian of Norwich and perhaps surprised to find these closely paralleled in the evangelical hymns of William Cowper. Some will find the practical and earthy wisdom of Brother Lawrence their most helpful guide. Others will be challenged by the austere but humane holiness of John Calvin and may find that paralleled in Ignatius Loyola. Others will find their footsteps quickened by the vivid imagery of the Carmelite Teresa and thrill to the same quality in the Puritan Bunyan. Some will find the splendour of ornate worship a help towards God, others will thrive best in silence and simplicity.

Yet this is not to advocate a 'pick and mix' approach, which is why the place of the Bible is so vital. Indeed all that variety is an echo of the marvellous variety of Scripture itself. Its story, poetry, psalmody, argument, passion, mystery, its depths and heights bear witness to the beauty and mystery of the many-splendoured grace of God. By the Bible, not simply as the Word God once spoke, but the Word he is speaking now, we will realize that no one kind of spirituality is a panacea and that each is to be judged solely by its influence on our walk with God.

It is likely that as we travel the Christian journey certain authors will become our regular companions. We shall have to be careful to be critical of them in the best sense of that word and while grateful to them hear beyond them the voice of Christ himself. Some of the implications of this will be explored further in Chapter 6.

But how does all this travelling hopefully relate to the arrival? 'He will continue to deliver us' says our text. Now that has an obvious surface meaning. Just as he has rescued us in past difficulties so he will continue to be our protector in future problems. But there is a deeper meaning. Paul, as so often, is thinking about final salvation, the end of all things when the 'not yet' becomes the 'now' and the goal of pilgrimage is reached.

It is fascinating that the metaphor that Paul uses in the letters to the Corinthians to speak of the glory of the arrival is one of growth and dynamism: 'So it will be with the resurrection of the dead. The body that is sown is perishable, it is raised imperishable; it is sown in dishonour, it is raised in glory, it is sown in weakness, it is raised in power' (1 Corinthians 15.42-43). The seed does not look like the plant, it comes to an end of one mode of existence but what emerges is in organic continuity and contained within what was sown. As we look at the glory of the spring countryside with the vigorous life bursting out of the tomb of the wintry earth we have a partial glimpse of the glory of the resurrection event. Paul strains language to breaking point here as he speaks of the coming of the kingdom: 'For the trumpet will sound, the dead will be raised imperishable and we will be changed' (v. 52). All the imperfections and blemishes of mortal life and pilgrimage will be swallowed up in the glory and excitement of the arrival.

Yet it is just at this very point that Paul brings us back to the present realities of pilgrimage. Since you have been called by God, the Creator of this amazing universe, and since he has committed himself to you with promises that he cannot break, the arrival is certain and glorious beyond imagining. But the effect of all this is not to make pilgrims into impractical visionaries: 'Therefore my dear brothers, stand firm. Let nothing move you. Always give yourself fully to the work of the Lord because you know that your labour in the Lord is not in vain' (v. 58). Rather the glory of the arrival is what alone makes it possible to travel hopefully. Far from the arrival being an anticlimax it is the reality of what awaits us on the arrival which is experienced partially on the journey. That means we have the strongest possible motivation to continue our journey and devote ourselves to the Lord's work.

There are two more observations to make before I come to the end of my first chapter. The first is that pilgrimage raises very acutely the question of guidance. Believing in the certainty of God's call does not mean we are transported in a robot-like fashion. More will be said about this in Chapter 3. At the moment what matters is that we realize that God is intimately concerned in our stories and we must be open to him.

The other is that what we are called to is an adventure. All the instincts deep in our nature which thrill to romance, heroism, mystery, risk and exciting new ventures are longings for what only God can give us. 'You have made us for yourself', said Augustine. The word translated 'for' is literally 'towards', and contains the idea of pilgrimage. As we shall see, the pilgrims whom we admire are not perfect, they failed, often badly, but nevertheless they left the old securities and with their eyes fixed on the goal pressed on to the heavenly city.

TWO

With God into the unknown: Abraham and the leap of faith

Genesis 11.26–12.9

After Terah had lived 70 years, he became the father of Abram, Nahor and Haran.

This is the account of Terah.

Terah became the father of Abram, Nahor and Haran. And Haran became the father of Lot. While his father Terah was still alive, Haran died in Ur of the Chaldeans in the land of his birth. Abram and Nahor both married. The name of Abram's wife was Sarai, and the name of Nahor's wife was Milcah; she was the daughter of Haran, the father of both Milcah and Iscah. Now Sarai was barren; she had no children.

Terah took his son Abram, his grandson Lot son of Haran, and his daughter-in-law Sarai, the wife of his son Abram, and together they set out from Ur of the Chaldeans to go to Canaan. But when they came to Haran, they settled there.

Terah lived 205 years, and he died in Haran.

THE CALL OF ABRAM

The Lord had said to Abram, 'Leave your country, your people and your father's household and go to the land I will show you.

> I will make you into a great nation
>> and I will bless you;
> I will make your name great,
>> and you will be a blessing
> I will bless those who bless you,
>> and whoever curses you I will curse;
> and all peoples on earth
>> will be blessed through you.'

So Abram left, as the Lord had told him, and Lot went with him. Abram was seventy-five years old when he set out from Haran. He took his wife Sarai, his Nephew Lot, all the possessions they had accumulated and the people they had acquired in Haran, and they set out for the land of Canaan, and they arrived there.

Abram travelled through the land as far as the site of the great tree of Moreh at Shechem. The Canaanites were then in the land, but the Lord appeared to Abram and said, 'To your offspring I will give this land.' So he built an altar there to the Lord, who had appeared to him.

From there he went on towards the hills east of Bethel and pitched his tent, with Bethel on the west and Ai on the east. There he built an altar to the Lord and called on the name of the Lord. Then Abram set out and continued towards the Negev.

Hebrews 11.8–16

By faith Abraham, when called to go to a place he would later receive as his inheritance, obeyed and went, even though he did not know where he was going. By faith he made his home in the promised land like a stranger in a foreign country, he lived in tents, as did Isaac and Jacob, who were heirs with him of the same promise. For he was looking forward to the city with foundations, whose architect and builder is God.

By faith Abraham, even though he was past age – and Sarah herself was barren – was enabled to become a father because he considered him faithful who had made the promise. And so from this one man, and he as good as dead, came descendants as numerous as the stars in the sky and as countless as the sand on the sea shore.

All those people were still living by faith when they died. They did not receive the things promised; they only saw him and welcomed them from a distance. And they admitted that they were aliens and strangers on earth. People who say such things show that they are looking for a country of their own. If they had been thinking of the country they had left, they would have had opportunity to return. Instead, they were longing for a better country – a heavenly one. Therefore God is not ashamed to be called their God for he has prepared a city for them.

Leaving home can be an exciting experience. Particularly when we are young and going off to university, a new job or a year's travel, the world seems a new and beckoning place. No more of the rules and regulations of home, the predictable domestic routines, the sense of being a child; all this will be left behind as we start on a fascinating journey of discovery and fulfilment. We know that often this is illusory; there is homesickness and disillusionment and often the constraints of the new life turn out to be as irksome as the old. Yet, on the whole, leaving home when we are young, is an exciting and necessary part of our growth as people.

When we turn to our first biblical story of pilgrimage we find that it begins with just such an experience of leaving home and all the familiar certainties. Yet there is one significant difference; Abraham is no youngster with most of life stretching out before him. He is a mature, settled man, just at that time of life when people are enjoying the comfortable feeling that comes from having put down roots and being part of a familiar and stimulating community. So often, however, the call of God to pilgrimage comes at just such a time to just such a person. Career is developing nicely, the mortgage is well on the way to being paid up, the children are happily settled at school and then comes the insistent voice: 'Leave your country, your people and your father's household and go to the land I will show you' (Genesis 12.1).

Because this story is familiar it is easy to miss the breathtaking nature of the events. It is told in a terse manner and we have to listen for clues to find out what the story is saying to us. We are in fact witnessing one of those moments where a climactic event takes place and nothing will ever be the same again. We shall concentrate mainly on a few verses in Genesis 11 and 12 and in Hebrews 11 and will explore what this archetypal story of pilgrimage has to say to our own stories. The Genesis passage concentrates on God's initiative in calling Abraham to pilgrimage and the Hebrews passages focuses on Abraham's response of faith, and it is the interplay of these which lies at the heart of the story.

What is happening here in fact is nothing less than a new creation; Abraham's pilgrimage is no mere nomadic journey of a group of wanderers, it is an event which compares in significance to the original act of making the worlds. Just as in Genesis 1 life bursts into its myriad forms when God speaks, so here once again God's speaking calls into existence a pilgrim people who are to be more numerous than the stars in heaven and the sand on the seashore. Just as the primeval couple were told to be 'fruitful and increase in number and fill the earth' (Genesis 1.28) so Abraham is promised descendants. Just as Adam and Eve are to

be stewards of the earth, so Abraham is promised a
land and indeed all the lands, to be peopled by his
posterity. Pilgrimage, then, is to be part of God's
own journey towards his chosen goal; it is to travel
with him and share his life. Already in this
pilgrimage in the grey dawn of human history
these guidelines are established.

Indeed pilgrimage begins further back still. In
Genesis 1—11 there are already fascinating hints
of the pilgrimage metaphor. In Genesis 3.6 we
read: 'Then the man and his wife heard the sound
of the Lord God as he was walking in the garden in
the cool of the day'. The idea is breath-taking.
God himself is inviting humans to walk beside him,
and a walk with God is no aimless stroll. This is in
essence what pilgrimage is about; it is walking
with God at his invitation and direction. Twice in
the story that follows the phrase is used: 'Enoch
walked with God' (5.22—23); 'Noah walked with
God' (6.9). Even after the Fall, pilgrimage is still
possible and, as we shall see, the imperfections of
pilgrims will not prevent them reaching the goal
nor fail to bring blessing to the whole world. That
is why it is so important to grasp that this is God's
pilgrimage. Without continually realizing that,
despair and disillusionment will soon set in. Thus,
I think, we best understand Abraham's actions
here as like those of Enoch and Noah. Like them
he is beginning a pilgrimage and travelling to a
city.

Now all that may fill us with dismay rather than
encouraging us, and we may feel that our own

fitful faith and erratic journey does not belong with these earth-shaking events. This is where the story-teller helps us to enter the world of Abraham by suggesting the very human and painful choices that had to be made, while the writer of the Letter to the Hebrews helps us to reflect on the deeper significance of these seemingly ordinary events. There are two aspects here: Abraham's daring faith and Abraham's human failings.

We have already commented on the devastating effect of God's call to Abraham to abandon the familiar securities and launch into the unknown and it is worth reflecting a little further on this. The first thing to notice is that the call becomes progressively more specific and more demanding: 'Leave your country, your people and your father's household' (Genesis 12.3). Leaving his country would turn Abraham into a refugee, a landless exile without roots or identity. Leaving his people would be tougher still because that would in effect mean he could not carry the land with him. But in the culture of the time, 'father's household' was the real wrench. An individual hardly existed except in relation to his extended family and to leave all that for what most would no doubt see as a crazy whim required faith of an unusual degree. Also when we go to another place nowadays we have probably seen it on television. We have almost certainly at least studied detailed brochures about its lifestyle, customs, climate, geography and history. But for Abraham, the land beyond the great river was shrouded in mystery with only contradictory and dubious travellers' tales. 'He went, even though he did not know where he was going' (Hebrews 11.8).

It is fascinating, in fact, to see how the author of Hebrews takes all these unknowns and turns them into occasions of the triumph of faith. Abraham is given more space than anyone else in Hebrews 11, the chapter of the pilgrimage of faith. Abraham left his country and it was no ordinary country. For centuries before Abraham the great city of Ur with its brilliant culture, magnificent buildings and talented people had stood proudly on the Euphrates. To leave that for a tent in the desert seemed incomprehensible. Yet where is that city now? Lost to sight for millennia until its vanished glories were excavated by archaeologists early this century, and once again its ruins covered by the shifting desert sands. Yet in place of this Abraham is promised another country and city 'with foundations whose architect and builder is God' (Hebrews 11.10). He left his people but becomes the ancestor of a new people whom God is proud to call his very own (Hebrews 11.16). The painful sacrifice of leaving his 'father's household' is more than compensated for by his very special place in the family of God.

Hebrews goes out of its way to emphasize that this daring faith of Abraham is open to other pilgrims. This is the thrust of chapter 11.13–16 about all those who have gone on the pilgrimage of faith and become 'aliens and strangers on the earth'. We will notice too that most of these heroes and heroines of faith are anonymous — now as then the story of Abraham's faith is retold in countless lives. A girl, well-connected and expensively educated, gives herself for the relief of suffering in a remote and primitive village in the midst of a vicious civil war. A young man abandons a promising career for full-time ministry. Busy middle-aged people gladly give their time to work for Amnesty International, to run a youth club for difficult teenagers in a draughty church hall and other unsung, unglamorous activities which are at the heart of pilgrimage. In these and countless other ways the story of Abraham happens again. And these lie close to the basic meaning of Lent which is freeing ourselves from excessive dependence on externals and entering more fully into the way of the cross.

But we may still feel that Abraham's daring faith is something we admire in others, but only fitfully, if at all, achieve for ourselves. This is where the second aspect, which is Abraham's failure, is so relevant to us. When we read carefully the story of Abraham in Genesis 11—25 we find no stained glass window figure, but a very real and fallible human being. Hardly has Abraham made his tremendous leap of faith than he is scuttling off to Egypt and attempting to pass off his wife as his sister. Later in chapter 16 neither he nor Sarah play very creditable roles in the story of Hagar and Ishmael. Then again in Genesis 20 Abraham tries to pass Sarah off as his sister to King Abimelech one of the Canaanite kings. Now, of course, it is possible to find good excuses for all these actions. They come at moments of fear and doubt when it seems as if God's promises are not going to be fulfilled, and it looks as if initiatives must be taken to save the whole scheme from disaster. But to say that is to miss the point. As we are going to see, God will not be deflected from his purposes by human failures. It is not good people he calls on pilgrimage, it is people with open hearts.

This question of open hearts is worth pausing on for a little. Often we find biblical characters guilty of the most appalling lapses, which certainly have disastrous consequences. David, most notably, springs to mind with his lying, adultery and murder. Yet the final assessment is that they were people of faith. David's spectacular sin was followed by the most agonized repentance. The key appears to be the continual turning to God after failure; returning to the highroad of pilgrimage after dallying in the bypaths. So it is with Abraham. We read such phrases as 'Abram went up from Egypt to the Negev' (Genesis 13.1). This journey is not simply an itinerary. Abraham is leaving the splendour and luxury of Egypt for the stern disciplines of the desert. Abraham is in fact remaking a pilgrimage to the places where he first did business with God. When we compare Genesis 13.3–4 with Genesis 12.8–9 we find the significant places of Bethel and Ai associated with his early experiences of God.

Nor in all this should we forget or minimize the role of Sarah. Right at the beginning an obstacle is identified: 'Now Sarah was barren; she had no children' (Genesis 11.30). Faith is instantly needed and a further reason added to those already commented on for seeing this whole venture as one of incalculable risk. Now when we place Sarah's barrenness beside the promise – which echoes the primeval one – to be fruitful and fill the earth, we see again the subtlety of the story-teller. That had appeared to be destroyed by the Fall in Genesis 3, one of whose consequences was sterility and death. Yet in Genesis 4 Eve is to be filled with joy as she shares in the creating life of God with the exultant cry – 'I have brought forth a man' (Genesis 4.1). Like Eve, Sarah is to have a son, but a long and difficult pilgrimage is to begin. She is to be taken into Pharaoh's harem, be humiliated by Hagar and know all the unsettled existence and frustrations of a nomadic life.

What I think we must not do is fall into the error of asking which are the 'real' Abraham and Sarah. Are they the venerable figures of strong faith and courage or are they the fickle, scheming fallible humans? The truth is that they are both. As we travel on pilgrimage we are often painfully aware of just such a conflict within ourselves. Each of us could easily write two different life stories. One would record the successes, the gifts, the qualities and strengths. The other would record the failures, the inadequacies, the selfishness, petulance and conceit. Both would be true. No one has expressed this agonizing dichotomy better than Paul in Romans 7: 'So in my mind I am a slave to God's law, but in my sinful nature a slave to the law of sin'. Pilgrimage does not mean denying that our dark side exists rather it involves increasingly opening that darkness to the light of God; 'walking in the light', in fact, which is how 1 John 1.7 describes pilgrimage.

So far we have looked at the risks taken by Abraham and Sarah, but these should not blind us to the staggering fact that God himself took breathtaking risks as he launched this pilgrimage. Indeed creation itself is a divine 'risk' because by breathing his own life into creatures other than himself God gives to these creatures responsibility and thus the capacity to disobey him. We have already seen how three times God 'walking' with humans has been emphasized. Each of these three times is in fact a dark and foreboding moment: the Fall in Genesis 3, the spread of death in the primeval world in Genesis 5 and the brink of the Flood in Genesis 6. Indeed from Genesis 3—11 the risk appears not to have paid off. Greed, violence, blasphemy and murder stalk the infant world as humanity treks inexorably further and further from Eden. The ultimate act of impiety occurs in chapter 11 when humanity, flushed with arrogance, builds the city and 'the tower which reaches to the heavens'. Then just at that moment God launches his counter-attack and from that very area calls Abraham to leave the city of this world and travel into the unknown towards the city 'whose architect and builder is God'.

So the God who calls us to pilgrimage is no

remote absentee landlord who expects others to take risks while he remains aloof and untouched. As we shall see in our final study, he himself is to go on pilgrimage and experience in his own body all its suffering and hardship. All through the Abraham story we have little phrases which underline that this pilgrimage is one of partnership and relationship between God and Abraham, for instance, 'The Lord made a covenant with Abram' (15.18); 'walk before me . . .' (17.1); 'The Lord appeared to Abraham' (18.1); 'Abraham remained standing before the Lord' (18.22).

With all this in mind we can look now at the journey Abraham took. Genesis 12.5–6 gives us only the briefest glimpse of the pilgrimage which was probably along one of the ancient trade routes south through Damascus and along the Sea of Galilee. There is the suggestion of journeying by stages and calling at places such as Bethel which later are to have significant associations. Two features of Abraham's pilgrimage through the land of promise are important to notice and will give us further food for reflection.

The first is the mention of Abraham pitching his tent. Like much else in the story this has a simple literal meaning and refers to an everyday action. Yet it also has profound significance as an indication of Abraham's inner life and attitudes. This is picked up in Hebrews 11.9: 'By faith he made his home in the promised land like a stranger in a foreign country.' This was not an ostentatious asceticism: we have already seen how in his excursion to Egypt, Abraham showed he had the same longing for security and comfort as any of us. The key is in Hebrews 11.10: 'For he was looking forward to the city with foundations.' Pilgrimage must always look to the future goal otherwise the clamour of the contemporary will all but drown out the eternal. This will work in two ways. The everyday will become filled with literally eternal significance because everything we say, do and are will be part of our pilgrimage and our spirituality. Indeed the more we are devoted to the eternal city the harder we will try to play as full a part as possible in the matters of this world. On the other hand, the eternal world will cease simply to be something in the far distant future and become an increasing reality in our everyday lives. We will become increasingly attuned to the reality of God and what he is preparing for us.

The second thing Abraham does is to build an altar and 'call on the name of the Lord'. The faithful obedience which Abraham showed when he left Ur to live in tents could only be sustained by regular worship represented by the altar. The story hints at regular worship and the importance of tangible reminders of God's presence. So it is on our pilgrimage. To say that God is everywhere can easily become on excuse for avoiding him anywhere. We are human, we need special places, anniversaries and tangible signs to keep alive our worship of God. Like Abraham we need to build an altar; the altar of public worship, of regular private prayer, of diligent use of 'the means of grace'. Worship is the lifeblood of the pilgrim and we shall explore this further in our look at the psalms of pilgrimage.

We have seen how in this richly human story of Abraham and Sarah, God's grace has worked creatively with ordinary human material and made it into something beautiful and inspiring. This leads us finally to consider the breath-taking results of this pilgrimage. 'All peoples of the earth will be blessed through you' (Genesis 12.3). By this simple statement this ancient pilgrimage is linked with every pilgrimage and the blessings of God's creating love reach out to the remotest corners of time and space. Ultimately this blessing is to find fulfilment in the vision of Revelation 7.9: 'a great multitude that no one could count, from every nation, tribe, people and language, standing before the throne and in front of the Lamb'. Only in the new creation at the end of our pilgrimage will we finally come to the city and enjoy its blessings.

Abraham himself becomes the hero of faith, the archetypal pilgrim. We have already examined how this is treated by the author of Hebrews. Paul and James also look to Abraham as the classic example of the journey of faith. Having studied the story we are now in a better position to understand what they mean. The providence of God works not just in the great events of history, but in the innumerable choices and decisions made daily and without apparent fuss. Yet it is from just such choices that momentous consequences flow.

This gives to our own pilgrimages with all the monotonous routine and trivial tasks a profound significance. As we travel and worship so the possibilities of Abraham's pilgrimage become ours and we move with quickened steps to the city.

THREE

Guide me, O Thou Great Redeemer: the community's uncertain faith

Exodus 17

WATER FROM THE ROCK

The whole Israelite community set out from the Desert of Sin, travelling from place to place as the Lord commanded. They camped at Rephidim, but there was no water for the people to drink. So they quarrelled with Moses and said, 'Give us water to drink.'

Moses replied, 'Why do you quarrel with me? Why do you put the Lord to the test?'

But the people were thirsty for water there, and they grumbled against Moses. They said, 'Why did you bring us up out of Egypt to make us and our children and livestock die of thirst?'

Then Moses cried out to the Lord 'What am I to do with these people? They are almost ready to stone me.'

The Lord answered Moses, 'Walk on ahead of the people. Take with you some of the elders of Israel and take in your hand the staff with which you struck the Nile, and go. I will stand there before you by the rock at Horeb. Strike the rock and water will come out of it for the people to drink.' So Moses did this in the sight of the elders of Israel. And he called the place Massah and Meribah because the Israelites quarrelled and because they tested the Lord saying, 'Is the Lord among us or not?'

THE AMALEKITES DEFEATED

The Amalekites came and attacked the Israelites at Rephidim. Moses said to Joshua, 'Choose some of our men and go out to fight the Amalekites. Tomorrow I will stand on top of the hill with the staff of God in my hands.'

So Joshua fought the Amalekites as Moses had ordered, and Moses, Aaron and Hur went to the top of the hill. As long as Moses held up his hands, the Israelites were winning, but whenever he lowered his hands the Amalekites were winning. When Moses hands grew tired, they took a stone and put it under him and he sat on it. Aaron and Hur held his hands up – one on one side, one on the other – so that his hands remained steady till sunset. So Joshua overcame the Amalekite army with the sword.

Then the Lord said to Moses, 'Write this on a scroll as something to be remembered and make sure that Joshua hears it, because I will completely erase the memory of the Amalekites from under heaven.'

> Moses built an altar and called it The Lord
> is my Banner. He said, 'For hands were lifted
> up to the throne of the Lord. The Lord will
> be at war against the Amalekites from
> generation to generation.'

'When the sun rises', said the poet Blake, 'do you
not see a round disk of fire somewhat like a guinea?
O no, no, I see an innumerable company of the
heavenly host crying "Holy, Holy, Holy, is the
Lord God Almighty"' (A vision of the Last
Judgment). These famous lines encapsulate two
different ways of looking at the world: the way of
realism and the way of vision. Both are needed and
nowhere more than on the pilgrimage of faith.
This insight of Blake will help us to understand
something of the richness of Exodus 17 which is
our next study in our theme of pilgrimage.
   On one level it is a straightforward story, part
of a cluster of stories called the 'murmuring
stories' where the Israelites complain against
Moses for leading them into the desert. Just as
God provided manna and quails in chapter 16, so
here he provides water and protection. Yet
underneath there are rich depths of imagery and
many layers of meaning. These events are more
than simply historical happenings, they represent
the needs and dangers and opportunities of the life
of faith. Just as a window is both real glass and also
an opening to worlds beyond itself so are these
stories. George Herbert expresses this memorably:

A man that looks on glass,
  On it may stay his eye.
Or if he pleaseth through it pass,
  And then the heaven espy.
      ('The Elixer')

We shall do both. We shall 'stay our eyes' on the actual story, but also look beyond it to its larger meaning.

Exodus 17 is a window on part of the great community pilgrimage of God's people from Egypt to the promised land. In the story of Abraham and Sarah, although at many points we are conscious of the presence of others, the emphasis is on the solitary nature of the leap of faith. Here the emphasis is on the communal nature of pilgrimage. Both sides are crucially important.

Without the real personal commitment to pilgrimage, the rigours and trials of the journey will soon knock us off course. Without personal prayer, Bible study and looking for God's guidance our faith will rapidly wither. Without faith being at the heart of our daily lives we shall easily be side-tracked from pilgrimage. As we have seen in the story of Abraham this does not mean we are perfect or that our faith is always pure and intense, rather it means that we are open to God. Each of us has our own road to travel, our own cross to carry, our own temptations and battles.

But what this story emphasizes is that no one is called to pilgrimage without becoming part of the great family of faith. This is underlined in

verse 1: 'The whole Israelite community set
out . . .' Thus we must learn from other pilgrims.
Sometimes this will be in the fellowship of God's
people with all its strength and stimulus and yet
with all its potential for hurt, annoyance and
misunderstanding, and these are certainly fully
encountered in the story. It will also mean
drawing deeply from the experiences of past
pilgrims. This is what this book is about and we
shall explore this theme more fully in Chapter 6.

What does it means to be a community called to
pilgrimage? There is a fascinating interplay here
between what God does and what humans do; we
are not robots, our pilgrimage is not a tramline, at
every point there is freedom to respond and
indeed to disobey. More particularly this story
focuses on three great necessities of pilgrimage:
the need for water, the need to fight and the need
to pray.

Both Exodus 16 and 17 emphasize that the basic
needs of bread and water are fundamental on
pilgrimage. On the literal level we must forget our
need for a cold drink on a hot day in this country
and imagine rather the inescapable enervating heat
of an eastern midday. We must further imagine
this encampment with children sticky and
truculent, tempers fraying, the smells and clutter
of a community on the move and then we see that
this is literally a matter of life and death. But on
another level this longing for water is a symbol of
that deeper thirst and hunger for God himself: 'As
the deer pants for streams of water, so my soul

pants for you, O God. My soul thirsts for God, for the living God' (Psalm 42.1, 2). Indeed a river, which is the presence of God, flows through the Bible and it is by drawing from that river that we grow in the faith and are able to continue the journey. The story begins with the river which flows through Eden and culminates with that same river watering the heavenly city. It surfaces in Psalm 46 as 'a river whose streams make glad the city of God'. In John 7, Jesus identifies it with the living Spirit: 'Whoever believes in me, as the scripture has said, streams of living water will flow from within him' (v. 38).

Perhaps few things also illustrate more effectively this interplay of God's will and human responsibility which lie at the heart of this story. Water is supplied by God alone and yet he uses Moses' staff as his immediate agent. It is to the examination of these issues we now turn.

First, only God can supply water. This is emphasized in verse 2: 'So they quarrelled with Moses and said ''Give us water to drink''. Moses replied, ''Why do you quarrel with me? Why do you put the Lord to the test?'' '

Moses is pointing out starkly that only God can be depended on in the desert where there are no visible and external props to faith. The people's quarrel was not with Moses' leadership but was a lack of faith in God as Creator. Water was one of the main signs of life and thus some of the main evidences that the Creator was at work. There are many times on pilgrimage when situations like this occur; we have, we believe, been called by God and yet he has led us into a cul-de-sac. We do not see how he can meet our need so we panic and we blame others, we blame circumstances and our vision fails.

It is vision, in fact, which is vital at moments like these. Vision is not seeing what is not there, vision is seeing all that is there. The thirst was real, the desert was real, but so also was the presence of God. The difference was that the presence of God was discerned only by the eye of vision. The letter to the Hebrews, speaking of Moses, captures this in a wonderful phrase: 'He persevered because he saw him who is invisible' (Hebrews 11.27). It is not that thirst can be conjured away but rather that the resources to meet it are there, but not yet visible.

Yet God uses a very ordinary object as his means of supplying water. God said to Moses: 'Walk on ahead of the people. Take with you some of the elders of Israel and take in your hands the staff with which you struck the Nile and go. I will stand before you by the rock at Horeb. Strike the rock, and water will come out of it and the people will drink' (Exodus 17.5–6). This is not simply a theatrical trick. God is reminding both Moses and the people in the most vivid and memorable way both of his mighty acts and of how important the human response to these was. The staff first appears in chapter 4 of Exodus in the mysterious incident where it becomes a snake, and then in chapter 7 Moses is ordered to strike the Nile with it, and the river changes into blood. It is significant that in chapter 8 verse 1 this incident is described as one in which 'The Lord struck the Nile'. At the heart of all these Exodus accounts is the creating and destroying power of God and the importance of a response of faith. This is underlined in verse 7 of our chapter: 'And he called the place Massah and Meribah because the Israelites quarrelled and because they tested the Lord saying, "Is the Lord among us or not?"'' God himself identifies our deepest needs and satisfies these, helping our faith by using methods which have demonstrated his power in the past. He adapts himself to our perception and helps our fitful faith.

But there are deeper levels still in this first incident about the water. This particular story is used by Paul in 1 Corinthians in the course of a discussion of warnings from Israel's history to the Christians then and, by implication, now. He compares the Exodus and the divine guidance by the cloud to baptism and then goes on: 'They all ate the same spiritual food and drank the same spiritual drink: for they drank from the spiritual rock that accompanied them, and that rock was Christ' (vv. 3 and 4). This wonderfully brings together the physical and the spiritual. These people literally wandered in the desert and literally drank water which gushed from the rock at Horeb. But in so doing, as in eating the literal manna, they were sharing in the life of the God they called Yahweh who now at 'the fulfilment of the ages' has revealed himself as

Jesus Christ. It is fascinating to notice how the phrase 'that rock was Christ' anticipates that better known one in 1 Corinthians 11.24 'This is my body'. Again the physical action of eating and drinking becomes a sharing of the life of God. The physical mirrors the spiritual and by the tangible actions of taking and eating, the intangible love of God becomes more real. So it is often that the physical action of pilgrimage can make the inner journey more real. The need for water is nothing less than the need for God himself, and as we continue to explore Exodus 17 we shall look at two ways in which this need is expressed, the need to fight and the need to pray.

Immediately this incident of the water is followed by one of fighting,[2] and this is a reminder of the need for continual vigilance. Probably this attack, a surprise and cowardly one, took place at some desert oasis. Once again the story is full of hidden depths of meaning. The Amalekites were descended from Esau and are first mentioned in a list of his descendants in Genesis 36.12. This links them with an age-old feud and reminds us again of how realistic and human these stories are.

The first thing to notice is that pilgrimage will involve fighting, it is not a holiday trip. The spiritual classics remind us often of this. Teresa of Avila speaks of the snakes and other unpleasant creatures which infest the entrance to the interior castle. Bunyan speaks of Apollyon and the other 'hobgoblins and foul fiends' which attack the pilgrim in the Valley of the Shadow. The pilgrim way is one of perpetual battling and wrestling and we cannot expect to avoid this in our own pilgrimage.

But alongside this we must notice how dreadfully this image of the Christian life has been misused. The right idea that fighting is a necessary part of Christian living has been perverted into the evil idea that it is God's will for his self-appointed defenders to massacre their opponent. Sadly it is all but too easy to find examples. One of the most disgraceful is the long and chilling history of Christian persecution of the Jews, an issue I return to later in this book. Just as unsavoury have been the innumerable wars of religion where different branches of the Christian Church have torn each other apart, have burned, pillaged, robbed and massacred in the name of the Prince of peace. We can think too of the Crusades where much energy was spent murdering each other rather than liberating the Holy Places. No branch of the Church has cause to be proud of the violent episodes in our history.

It is also important to remember that we in the late twentieth century in the Western Church are by no means immune from this violent and overbearing spirit. Phrases such as 'contend for the faith' (Jude 3) are often taken to mean that our conduct is to be marked by truculence, aggressiveness and rudeness. We interpret different styles and different kinds of language as fundamental differences and are always sniffing out heresy and error. There are few images of the

Christian life, it seems, more easy to abuse than that of fighting.

How, then, can we use this image in a positive way? I think two things need to be said. First of all, when we are reading Old Testament history we need to remember that ancient Israel was a political entity as well as God's covenant people. We cannot therefore simply transfer what is appropriate for a nation state in the ancient world to the experience of the Christian Church. Moreover, we are here dealing with unique events, God's 'mighty acts' which created the nation of Israel and we cannot simply claim Divine sanction for our own causes.

The second thing is that we have to fight the real enemy. That real enemy's identity is spelled out in Ephesians 6.10ff: 'For our struggle is not against flesh and blood, but against the rulers, against the authorities, against the powers of this dark world and against the spiritual forces of evil in the heavenly realms' (v. 12). This means that not only is killing mortal enemies wrong, it is pointless. The real enemy is not being touched. Thus this incident of fighting is a symbol of our fight with the powers of evil who lie in wait for us at every stage of our pilgrimage.[3]

Thus the fight is real and arduous. Many enemies such as laziness, apathy, sinfulness and the powers of darkness have to be strenuously fought with daily 'taking up the cross'. Lent reminds us of the need to travel light and thus be mobile and ready to deal with our enemies. Lent is

41

not to be trivialized into giving up chocolate, but is a time when we reassess our priorities and more firmly resolve to go on to fight the Lord's battles.

Once again, as in the water incident, there is a blend of God's providence and human responsibility. The verse which controls this aspect of the whole Exodus narrative is 14.14: 'The Lord will fight for you, you need only be still.' This is underlined in our chapter here in verse 16: 'The Lord will be at war against the Amalekites from generation to generation.'

This becomes part of the age-old battle in which God has already committed himself against the powers of darkness. 'And I will put enmity between you and the woman, and between your offspring and hers; he will crush your head, and you will strike her heel' (Genesis 3.15). Since God is battling against evil, his people, under his guidance, are also involved in that battle. In this story that is illustrated by Joshua's military leadership.

The desert is the place of spiritual discipline and testing. The fundamental need of water, both physical and spiritual, is the first great insight of this chapter. The need to fight against all evil powers who try to destroy us or at least deflect us from pilgrimage is the next. Now we turn to the third great necessity which is prayer, and this binds the other two together.

The need of prayer is what lies behind the curious little incident of Moses sitting on the hill, holding the staff of God in his hands.

Commentators differ widely, even extravagantly, in their interpretation of this passage. Some argue in a very literal way that this is simply a signal to begin the battle. This, however, hardly fits with the ebb and flow of Israel's success, and the need for Aaron and Hur to hold up his hands until the battle was over. Others, with more imagination, at least, have argued that here Moses is acting as a kind of cult magician and that the staff has miraculous powers. I think the reality is more complex and has to do with the power of prayer.

The first significant fact to notice is that the word prayer is not mentioned, because prayer is not so much one activity among others as the whole atmosphere and content in which everything else happens. Lifting up hands is a common gesture to symbolize prayer, and in this incident lowered hands symbolizes the temporary cessation of prayer. From many passages, one or two can be cited: 'In your name I will lift up my hands' (Psalm 63.4) and: 'I want men everywhere to lift up holy hands in prayer, without anger or disputing' (1 Timothy 2.8). Like Abraham's tent and altar, the uplifted hands were tangible symbols reflecting reality.

I think this is an important feature of prayer. We can pray anywhere, we can pray without words, we can pray without preparation. However, for that continuous life of prayer to be real there must be times when it is focused and at such times external factors are important. This may be a special place, a particular time of the day, even a particular posture. None of these makes God more ready to listen than he is already but they are enormous helps to us in creating the right kind of atmosphere in which we may more readily hear his voice. A missionary told a story of how some new converts in a remote village were extremely anxious to take prayer seriously. Each of them chose a remote spot, and as time passed the tracks to each of these places became clearly marked. They also agreed to help each other to keep up this practice by checking each other's paths to make sure that they were not becoming overgrown and thus indicating neglect of prayer. Of course, this could easily become mechanical, but praying is difficult and anything that helps, as here Aaron and Hur holding up Moses' hands, is not to be despised.

This leads on to another consideration which is the relation of the Israelite victory to the prayer of Moses. We have already looked at the subtle interplay of God's providence and human response throughout this chapter and nowhere is this more vital than in the whole question of intercessory prayer. To put it bluntly: Why pray if God already plans? And also, is there not some presumption in this kind of prayer? Does it not imply that we know better than God and that we have to persuade him to do what he is reluctant to do? A striking verse in Philippians 4.6 encapsulates the problem: 'Do not be anxious about anything, but in everything, by prayer and petition, with thanksgiving, present your requests to God.'

What this verse appears to be saying is that we have to tell God, or at least remind him, what our requests are. It makes no sense, it contradicts all we know about God's perfect wisdom and knowledge. And yet the Bible persistently from beginning to end tells us to pray, our own instincts confirm this and, whatever theoretical difficulties there may be when we are in trouble, we pray. We know, of course, that there are other kinds of prayer: praise, thanksgiving, confession and so on, but the particular kind of prayer that concerns us now is intercession.

The real problem with the apparently logical dismissal of intercessory prayer is that it sees God as operating a purely mechanical universe in which iron laws of cause and effect operate. God is seen as starting off processes and occasionally intervening if part of the machinery goes wrong. But the biblical doctrine of creation is not just that God created heaven and earth 'in the beginning', but that creation is going on now and that he is active in every part of the world he has made. In such a world, prayer no longer is seen as a mechanical or even magical activity. Rather it is one of the ways in which God works out his loving purposes. Our prayers become part of his ordering of events. Prayer is not simply an attitude, it is also something we do; a situation prayed over is not the same as one where no prayer has happened. Prayer indeed allows us to co-operate with God as he is at work in the world.

It is much more helpful, I find, to think of

God's creating love in terms of a dramatist or novelist. A great creative artist, as he writes a play or a novel, has complete control over his characters, the stories of their lives and the words which they utter. Yet such authors will often say that the characters take a life of their own and more or less write their own parts.[4] That blend of control and room for response and growth is at the very heart of what prayer is about.

So in situations of conflict, prayer is not an optional extra but part of what is done about the situation. It is not an alternative to doing, it is part of the action. If we pray about the success of an examination or an interview we still have to sit the one and attend the other. Above all it is about relationship. It is our growing knowledge of God and his ways. It is the hearing his voice and taking risks as he leads us on to new experiences.

Of significance as well is the place where this prayer happened. It took place on a hilltop, a literal part of the landscape and probably the mountain of revelation known as Sinai and Horeb. Like everything else in this story this exists on various levels. The mountain is a sacred place, at once desert and altar.[5] It is a place of silence and loneliness where the voice of God can be heard without distraction. The call of pilgrimage is the call to scale the mountain as we shall see both in our study of the Ascent Psalms and of Mary's hurried journey through the hill country of Judaea.

As we pause for a moment to look back at what Exodus 17 says about the community's pilgrimage

two observations can be made. The first is the
importance of vision for pilgrimage, of being able
to see through the inner realities and significance
beyond the apparent meaningless of much of our
daily lives. To see in hurts, slights and conflicts
opportunities for growth. To see in the often drab
routine possibilities of new life and to find wells of
water springing up in unexpected places. The
second is a clearer picture of what are the real
needs of a community on pilgrimage. These
necessities are basically simple, but, as we have
seen are windows on to much greater realities. All
of them have shown us the need both to receive
and actively to use what we have received, to face
reality and yet see beyond that to the realms of
vision and to glimpse the kingdom.

FOUR

The steep ascent: the community's songs of pilgrimage

Psalm 129
A song of ascents

They have greatly oppressed me from my
     youth —
  let Israel say —
they have greatly oppressed me from my
     youth,
  but they have not gained the victory over
    me.
Ploughmen have ploughed my back
  and made their furrows long.
But the LORD is righteous;
  he has cut me free from the cords of the
    wicked.

May all who hate Zion be turned back in
     shame.
May they be like grass on the housetops,
  which withers before it can grow;
with it the reaper cannot fill his hands,
  nor the one who gathers fill his arms.
May those who pass by not say,
   'The blessing of the LORD be upon you;
   we bless you in the name of the LORD.'

Psalm 130
A song of ascents

Out of the depths I cry to you, O LORD
    O Lord, hear my voice.
Let your ears be attentive
    to my cry for mercy.

If you, O LORD, kept a record of sins,
    O Lord, who could stand?
But with you there is forgiveness;
    therefore you are feared.

I wait for the LORD, my soul waits,
    and in his word I put my hope.
My soul waits for the Lord
    more than watchmen wait for the morn-
      ing,
    more than watchmen wait for the morning.

O Israel, put your hope in the LORD,
    for with the LORD is unfailing love
    and with him is full redemption.
He himself will redeem Israel from all their
    sins.

Psalm 131
A song of ascents. Of David

My heart is not proud, O LORD,
    my eyes are not haughty;
I do not concern myself with great matters.

or things too wonderful for me.
But I have stilled and quieted my soul;
   like a weaned child with its mother,
   like a weaned child is my soul within me.

O Israel, put your hope in the LORD
   both now and for evermore.

Music shares with other arts the power to transform our immediate surroundings and open up new and different worlds. It has the capacity to create before us the chilly depths of a Swedish pine forest, the nostalgic landscapes of rural England, the beat of waves on a Hebridean shore, the bustle of a market day in the Urals, the splendour of the night sky and indeed every conceivable place and experience. Thus in our exploration of the theme of pilgrimage we turn now to the Psalms which have a similar variety of mood and setting, encompassing the whole gamut of human experience. In particular the Psalter expresses the emotions and feelings of the pilgrim people of God and, though rooted in particular times and places, speaks to pilgrims in circumstances far removed from those who originally wrote and sang these songs.

   The main focus of our thoughts will be a group of fifteen psalms (120—134), and within that, Psalms 129—131. This particular group is linked by the common title 'Song of Ascents'. Some have argued that this refers to the literary structure with a 'step-like' repetition of words and phrases in successive verses. This may be, but it is not peculiar to this part of the Psalter. A more likely suggestion is that these 'Songs of Ascents' were sung by pilgrims on their way to Jerusalem for the great festivals of the Jewish year. The Hebrew word translated 'ascent' or 'going up' is used elsewhere in the Psalter for going on pilgrimage to the temple: 'who shall ascend the hill of the Lord and who shall stand in his holy place?' (Psalm 24.3).

When we look at the beginning and ending of this group of psalms a pattern begins to emerge. In Psalm 120.5 the psalmist laments: 'Woe to me that I dwell in Meshech, that I live among the tents of Kedar.' Meshech was on the edge of the Caspian Sea and Kedar was in the South Arabian desert; two locations which would be at the extremes of your geographical horizons at that time. Psalm 134 is a little vignette of the perpetual praise of God in Zion. Thus, starting from whatever extreme point of the compass we may happen to be, the pilgrimage ultimately leads to 'Zion, city of our God'.

Moreover, as we shall see, this journey is not mere geography. Anyone who has travelled into Jerusalem from the Judaean highlands knows that in strictly literal terms the road goes 'down' to Jerusalem. Yet this insignificant little hill of Zion, crowned by its citadel captured by King David, becomes the 'joy of the whole earth', 'the city of the great King' (Psalm 48.2). All of us have places which are particularly special to us and the journey to these is marked by eager anticipation as the familiar landmarks slip past and the moment comes, often repeated but always fresh, when the well-loved place comes into view. One of my own particular delights is leaving the M6 just south of Birmingham and driving deep into the Warwickshire countryside, passing places with romantic names such as Charlecote Lucy and Aston Cantlow until the spire of Holy Trinity Church, burial place of Shakespeare, looms above the landscape and the thrill of being in Stratford-upon-Avon again becomes a reality. That gives some idea of the excitement of the pilgrims, as Jerusalem with its temple towering above the city walls burst on their sight. This delight would be all the greater given the hazards of the journey. The pilgrims would travel in constant danger from bandits, wild beasts, rough roads, hunger and thirst. This has been a constant feature of pilgrimage through the ages. In our world of motorway service stations and fast and easy transport it is salutary to remember the faith and courage of those who travelled by foot, sleeping by the roadside or in verminous and dangerous inns not knowing if they would ever reach their destination, still less if they would return. It is such pilgrims who sing of their journey in this group of psalms which become part of the songs of all those travelling to 'the city whose builder and architect is God'.

A further noteworthy feature of this group of psalms is that they can usefully be divided into five groups of three, each of which mirrors on a smaller scale of pilgrimage from Meshech/Kedar to Zion.¹ I want now to look more closely at one of these triads (Psalms 129—131) and at what I have called the 'steep ascent', borrowing the phrase from Bishop Heber's hymn on the dangers and hardships of following Christ:

> They climbed the steep ascent of heaven,
> Through peril, toil and pain:
> O God to us may grace be given
> To follow in their train.
>> ('The Son of God goes forth to war')

Psalm 129 begins with oppression and hardship and Psalm 131 ends with perpetual hope in God. The three psalms express the harsh realities of pilgrimage in our fallen world. Each of the three psalms has a hinge where the mood changes: 'But the Lord is righteous, he has cut me free' (129.4); 'But with you there is forgiveness' (130.4); 'But I have stilled and quietened my soul' (131.2). There is a development here from the earlier Songs of Ascents where the hardships and obstacles had been physical: sunstroke and moon madness (121.6); floods; attacks by wild animals and traps (124.6-7). Now they become much more inner problems, reminding us that the journey is inward as well as outward. This is one of the most significant factors about pilgrimage. The pilgrim is journeying on different levels. There is the level of everyday routine: the normal business of eating, sleeping, work, leisure and the mixture of the ordinary and the unexpected. There is the spiritual counterpart of this: the daily use of the 'means of grace', public worship, fellowship and the defeats and victories of the life of faith. Bringing all these together is a major concern of pilgrimage, as is the effort to see all life as a pilgrimage. The psalms we shall look at do this very successfully largely by using very physical images to suggest spiritual hazards; the difficulties are not 'all in the mind'. Also there is real progress in these psalms: 129 and 130 deal with two inescapable hazards of pilgrimage and 131 deals with its goal.

The particular thrust of Psalm 129 is that hardship is inevitable. Part of this is, of course, the natural lot of humankind. We live in an uncertain world where every day a phone call, a letter, a visit brings tragic news to someone. But the word 'oppressed' in verse 1 also suggests the kinds of hardship that are part of being a pilgrim. Indeed this is one of the most distressing aspects of the life of faith. For many years a woman cares for an elderly parent, receiving little but ingratitude and complaints. At the end of it she finds herself 'left on the shelf', with life seeming to have passed her by. A young mother is left with growing children when her husband dies of a heart attack shortly after having given up a comfortable home and a promising career to take up full-time ministry. The life of faith is full of these situations: God calls people and then seems to abandon them to struggle alone on their pilgrimage.

One very striking example of this is the story of

the pioneer missionary John Paton. Paton, originally from Dumfries, was a gifted young man who volunteered to serve with the New Hebrides Mission. At that time, in the 1850s, the New Hebrides group of islands, about a thousand miles from New Zealand, were inhabited by cannibals, and the sick, old and very young were frequently abandoned to death. Paton and his wife, however, went there with great confidence and assurance that God would protect them. Sadly they had hardly arrived on the island of Tanna when their troubles began. People blamed them for droughts and for heavy rains and stole from them. Worse still, the site of their house was unhealthy and soon they were attacked by fever. Then the heaviest blow of all fell. Ten months after their arrival, John Paton was overjoyed when his wife gave birth to a son. The tide seemed to have turned and God was smiling on them again. A mere five weeks later, mother and baby both died of fever leaving Paton alone and desolate. Something of his agony can be sensed in his diary: 'I built the grave round and round with coral blocks, and covered the top with beautiful white coral, broken small as gravel; and that spot became my sacred and much-frequented shrine . . . But for Jesus and the fellowship he vouchsafed me there, I must have gone mad and died beside that lonely grave.' That is so often the story of pilgrimage and a multitude of other examples could be given from the lives of 'ordinary' pilgrims as well as the famous.

Psalm 129 is a community song and the psalmist here is speaking for the nation and reflecting on Israel's own difficult and dangerous journey. He goes right back to their origins – 'Sorely have they afflicted me from my youth' (v. 2). There was another perfect illustration of the dashing of high hopes when the sons of Jacob arrived in Egypt and they enjoyed the protection of Joseph, now Pharaoh's second-in-command. Then as time passed they were reduced to the status of slaves. They were eventually rescued by God's intervention and began that uneasy pilgrimage through the desert. But even in the promised land wave after wave of conquerors punctuated the whole course of their history. Little wonder then that so many of the songs of this community's pilgrimage are laments and pleas to God to rescue them.

Even more significantly this Jewish pilgrimage is organically related to the Christian pilgrimage. Christians are part of that community of the faithful stretching back to Abraham and Moses. This makes it all the more necessary for Christians to repent of the awful history of anti-Semitism which has disfigured so much of Western history. Every time I visit York and pass the pleasant grassy mound on which Clifford's Tower stands, it is with a shudder that I remember the awful day in the eleventh century when Christians led by their priest massacred dozens of Jews who had taken refuge in an underground crypt in the church which once stood there. I write these words in the year which commemorates the fiftieth anniversary of the liberation of Auschwitz and reflect with deep sadness that the Holocaust grew out of the very heart of Western Christian civilization. This does not of course mean that the modern Israeli state has itself an unblemished record in relation to the Palestinians. What it does mean is that those who are themselves on pilgrimage must never succumb to the temptation to oppress other pilgrims.

Pilgrimage then can be a brutal experience and this song used very vivid imagery to express these hardships. 'The plowers ploughed upon my back, they made long their furrows.' The metaphor is gruesome: whips with pieces of bone or iron would leave long red marks on people's backs. Perhaps the modern phrase 'riding roughshod' over someone conveys something of the idea. The hardships of pilgrimage are real: you may have read *The Interior Castle* by Teresa of Avila and shuddered at the poisonous toads and vipers which impede the pilgrim, and somewhat similarly felt the fear of the 'hobgoblins' and 'foul fiends' in Bunyan's *Pilgrim's Progress*. No pilgrimage can avoid these hazards and opponents.

All this can easily lead either to apathy or despair. Is it worth continuing on pilgrimage at all? you may wonder. And at this point you may simply opt out and either lose interest or angrily say that neither the journey nor the destination match up to what the songs and stories of other pilgrims would have us believe. Yet in the midst of this agony the psalmist discerns a powerful current flowing in the opposite direction. 'But the Lord is righteous, he has cut me free from the cords of the wicked.' God has intervened to cut the ropes which are tied to the ploughs being driven over the pilgrims' backs. In particular the psalmist uses the name Yahweh, the name by which God is known as the Lord who has made a covenant with Israel and is committed to them by promises that he will not break.

Then he turns to the fate of the 'wicked'. These are not a separate class of people whom God has specially singled out for punishment. Rather these are the people who deliberately oppose God, or, to put it another way, turn their backs on the pilgrimage to Zion. It is important to notice that when the Bible speaks about judgement there is always an 'inbuilt repentance clause'. A good example here is Jonah who preaches 'In forty days Nineveh will be destroyed'. He says nothing about repentance and forgiveness. Yet the people of Nineveh do repent and God does forgive them. An illustration from everyday life might be as follows. You are walking along a pavement in a busy street and, deep in thought, you step out to cross the road. A bus is trundling towards you and someone yells 'Watch out!' They are not shouting at you so that the bus rolls on and crushes you under its wheels, but so that you can get out of the way.

What then does all this say about the life of pilgrimage? The concentration on the hardships gives a true sense of realism and of priorities, they prevent the pilgrims becoming so entranced with the journey that they lose sight of the goal. The other thing that becomes clear is that 'the righteous' and 'the wicked' are not so much two kinds of people as two kinds of basic attitude towards life and pilgrimage. The righteous are those who live an ultimately fruitful life as part of the pilgrim community. Righteousness in the Old Testament always has a social dimension because it involves right relationships with God and with each other. The wicked are those who cut themselves off from the Creator and thus become like weeds sprouting on flat roofs which have no time to grow before they are blasted by the elements.

But just as a comfortable feeling begins to grow another difficulty begins to emerge. Structures and systems opposed to God will vanish like weeds withering in the sun. This is most encouraging; God will protect me on pilgrimage and all my enemies will be dealt with. How easily, though, that can lead to an unpleasant complacency. I feel good and privileged, God has especially favoured me and I can look with secret or open contempt on others. By doing so I have put myself into the position of being God's enemy. If even these outstanding pilgrims, Abraham and Moses, sometimes got it badly wrong who am I to expect I will get it right? There are going to be sins, blunders and often incredible stupidity. This is the situation envisaged in our next psalm. Just as Psalm 129 shows that hardship is inevitable, so Psalm 130 is a reminder that failure is inescapable.

Psalm 130 is especially appropriate for Lent and was adopted as one of the Penitential Psalms of the ancient church. There is a sense here of total alienation and of being cut off from God, not now because of oppression from God's enemies but because my own sins and failures have made me one of those enemies. 'Out of the depths' is the situation from which the psalmist cries. This is not just the equivalent of being 'down in the dumps'. The phrase is used in the Old Testament for the depths of the ocean, the land of primeval chaos called Sheol, the place of shadows and the dead. Once again, the best illustration of this is the story of Jonah. In his frantic attempt to escape his mission Jonah is swallowed by a fish and calls to God: 'from the depths of the grave I called for help. You hurled me into the deep, into the very heart of the sea' (Jonah 2.2–3). Instead of going on 'pilgrimage' to Nineveh Jonah had run away to Tarshish. Many people have tried to find out where Tarshish was, but the word may simply mean 'open sea', another way of saying that when we run away from God there is nowhere to go – indeed we will end up in Sheol. Before Christ's resurrection there was and could be no certainty that there was any way out of that realm. Yet this ancient pilgrim in Psalm 130, by a leap of faith, cries to God even from there.[2]

These depths are part of pilgrimage and the psalmist is deliberately general so that readers can fit their own particular darkness into what he says. There are times when a great black cloud lies over everything, you find no pleasure in your family and friends, your work has gone stale, your normal enjoyments have palled and you have a vague sense of inadequacy, vulnerability and guilt. What is important to notice here is that the psalmist, like Jonah, cries to the Lord. The repetition of different phrases – 'I cry . . .' 'hear my voice', 'let your ears be attentive' – shows that this is no casual request, it is an urgent insistent demand. It is a recognition that serious action is needed and that God must intervene.

The key to unlock this dungeon is God's mercy and forgiveness. This forgiveness is not a sentimental sloppiness which pats us on the head indulgently. This forgiveness is tough and bracing. The result of being forgiven is that God is feared. God accepts me unconditionally but that acceptance changes me and causes me to leave behind those attitudes of pride, selfishness, complacency and bitterness which caused me to become his enemy.

Jesus' story of the Pharisee and the Tax Collector in Luke 18.9–14 is a profound illustration of this. We all know the 'right' response to it. We rightly see the blatant self-parading of the Pharisee as he compares himself favourably to sinners of various kinds including the man praying beside him, and as he reminds God of his abstemious lifestyle and his generosity. So far so good. But let us pause. What about my prayers? Of course I know not to use words of self-congratulation and disparagement of others, but what about the real feelings behind the words, the bits I do not say and others do not hear? But God knows exactly how much vanity and conceit lurks so often behind my pious words and how appalled I would be if these were flashed up on a screen for everyone to see. And what about the tax collector? How easy it is to sentimentalize him as a stumbling, erring individual who had got it wrong but was really well-meaning and trying to do better. The idea lurks there that it was this man's good intentions and human weakness which appealed to God and made him predisposed to treat him kindly. But that will not do. If we want to find the modern equivalent of the tax collector we will find him in one of those loan sharks who prey on the vulnerability and desperation of the unemployed, the single parent, the teenager from a broken home, the frail and elderly in depressing housing estates. He was a vicious lout who would send the 'heavies' round to beat up the unfortunate who could not pay. But he had realized, unlike the Pharisee, that his only claim on God was his need and he had thrown himself on God's mercy. The Pharisee, on the other hand, admirable man as he was in many ways, essentially uses prayer to bargain with God and has no sense of his need for forgiveness. It is all too easy to slip into a similar attitude and begin to feel smirkingly superior to the Pharisee. I heard of a Sunday School teacher who told this story of the Pharisee and the tax collector, and at the end of it said to the children it was time to have a prayer and 'boys and girls, let's thank God that we're not like the Pharisee!'

One of the utmost difficult lessons to learn on pilgrimage is the sheer luxury of the unconditional forgiveness and grace of God. 'Fearing' God is not possible if I come to him with my own exploits, achievements and records of successes. If I do that I am really trying to bargain with him. What does the psalmist say is the answer to the feelings of guilt and the frantic desire to be in God's 'good books'? The words used are 'wait' and 'hope' and these point us to a new stage on the pilgrimage. These words can be misunderstood to suggest a mere passive hanging around or killing time, but that would be to miss the point. Rather the words suggest a reaching out of one's whole being to God and thus contain the pilgrimage idea. In the story of Abraham, pilgrimage was much more than getting from one place to another, and here waiting and hoping are much more than sitting back to see what happens. But what does this mean in practical terms? I think first it means keeping on diligently doing the normal tasks of daily living. Just as 'watchmen wait for the morning' it is important in Christian living to keep on at whatever responsibilities life brings us, realizing that these can be moments of revelation. It was after all while tending sheep that Moses had his vision of God. Also, the illustration of watchmen is a reminder of the importance of being alert and open to new possibilities and opportunities.

Thus pilgrimage can once again become life-giving and fruitful. This has been a recurring theme throughout the 'Ascent Psalms', for example, 'Those who sow in tears will reap with songs of joy' (126.5); 'You will eat the fruit of your labours; blessing and prosperity will be yours' (128.2). This is not because of the pilgrim's determination or goodness but because of God's 'unfailing love'. This love cannot be diminished by any failures on their part because 'with him is full redemption' (130.7). This is not just enough to deal with the particular 'depths' which inspired the psalm but 'He will redeem Israel from all their sins' (130.8). This means that all future failures and blunders will be covered by his grace as well. However, with the salutary experiences of hardship and failure this fact will not lead to complacency but to healthy and robust fear of the Lord which leads on to the next stage of pilgrimage.

This next stage is outlined in Psalm 131. It has already been noted how each group of three psalms in the 'Songs of Ascents' mirrors in miniature the structures of the entire group beginning in the gloom of Meshech/Kedar and ending in Zion. Thus in Psalm 122.6 the pilgrimage ends in 'the peace of Jerusalem', in 125.2 with the protecting mountains surrounding Jerusalem; in 128.5 with the prosperity of Jerusalem and at the end of the whole section in 134 with perpetual praise in the sanctuary. This particular group ends in Psalm 131 not with a specific mention of Zion but with a celebration of the reality of the presence of God which is what the city of God means. The danger of over-emphasizing any specific picture of the goal of pilgrimage such as city, home, choir or any other image of heaven is that we can easily imagine that this exhausts its meaning and thus lose that sense of wonder and mystery which is at the heart of true worship. I think Richard Baxter expresses this well:

> My knowledge of that life is small,
> The eye of faith is dim.
> I only know that Christ is there.
> And I will be with him.

With this assurance, just as on pilgrimage hardship is inevitable and failure inescapable, so peace is possible.

This peace comes first of all not from a change in the pilgrim's circumstances but a transformation in the pilgrim's heart. Once again the psalmist is showing a shrewd knowledge of human nature. The pilgrim suffers from the same tendency to pride as anyone else. Pride is not something characteristic of only a few conceited individuals. It is not simply pride in the natural human condition without the grace of God. This psalm gives us a wonderful anatomy of pride which is essentially creating an egocentric universe where everyone and everything are judged on how they affect me. This pride has two particular characteristics.

The first mark of pride is my overvaluation of myself – 'occupy myself with great matters and things too wonderful for me' (v. 1). How tempting it is to bring the conversation round to my exploits real and imagined. How ready I am to tell a story and repeat a conversation which shows me in a better light than is warranted. How glibly I tell of the devastating retort I wish I had made at the time but actually thought up an hour later. Ultimately this springs from a feeling of insecurity, a frantic fear that no one could possibly love me if they really knew what I was like. To compensate for this I create an idealized image of myself where I am always in control and know how to respond to every situation, never appear to be vulnerable and never allow myself to be at a loss. This feeling is particularly strong because it usually exaggerates real aspects of my personality. If I am assertive and aggressive I see this as strength, leadership and honesty. If I am compliant and easily led I see this as gentleness and caring concern. If I am aloof I see this as carefulness and self-control. If this kind of thing goes on I live more in a fantasy world and all my energy is devoted to maintaining this fantasy image. Now you may say this is a caricature, and perhaps it is. But I am deliberately putting the case strongly to make the point.

This is closely linked with the second aspect of pride which is to have 'haughty eyes' (v. 1), and that means looking down on and undervaluing others. Much of this springs from self-love: others' assertiveness is not conviction but arrogance, their concern is an unworthy desire to please, their discipline is aloofness and so on. We all know how painful this is when others do it to us and there are few things more calculated to destroy our peace of mind.

What is the answer to this cancerous pride which so often eats at the hearts of our Christian pilgrimage? The psalmist here says that is to luxuriate in the peace of God which accepts and loves us as we are. 'But' he says in verse 2, 'I am cultivating the secret of peace'. This does not simply mean 'peace' in the sense of the absence of hostility. The word which would best describe the thought of his verse is the great Hebrew term *shalom*, a positive and dynamic word which suggests a life lived and a journey travelled in harmony with God and his creation.

This is focused in the image of the 'weaned child' with its suggestions of both dependency and growth. Jesus more than once spoke of the need of becoming childlike in order to enter the kingdom of heaven. The kind of frantic pride which has already been discussed is not there in small children. There is instead an utter lack of self-consciousness and a playfulness as well as a total dependence on the parent. In that sense, the child becomes a model for the pilgrim and the raging turmoil of pride is replaced by calm assurance.

We must not, however, press this image too far. There are many ways in which it is very damaging for the pilgrim to be like a child. That is why the psalmist balances this picture of complete dependence and trust with one of responsibility: 'I have calmed and quieted my soul.' It is this blend of active determination and childlike trust which puts the peace back into pilgrimage.

But this is not yet the final goal and thus the psalmist says in v. 3, 'O Israel hope in the Lord from this time on and for evermore.' While on pilgrimage there will always be need for hope and trust. The hardships of Psalm 129 and the failures of Psalm 130 will not simply be left behind as a train passes through stations. They will always be a feature of pilgrimage and peace must be fought for.

This is why the psalmist urges Israel to hope not only in the present but 'for evermore'. There have been many arguments about what the Hebrew word *olam*, translated 'evermore', means exactly but these are not especially relevant to our concern. The word suggests having the quality of the life of God himself and not being subject to the accidents and failures of mortal living. Thus the peace of which the psalmist speaks is not simply the fleeting glimpses enjoyed from time to time on the journey but the homeland to which the pilgrim is travelling. Other ascent psalms have used such pictures as stability, prosperity, harvest, harmony and music to speak of that homeland, 'Zion, city of our God', and peace belongs with that attractive cluster.

I suggest already that thinking of the life of faith as a pilgrimage draws attention to the rich variety of the various traditions and also to deep underlying unity. This is what C. S. Lewis called 'Deep Church' which is neither 'high' nor 'low' but the profound unity of those engaged in the common journey towards the heavenly home. Peace does not mean that all pilgrims will be identical but it does mean that they will travel in harmony. It means realizing that not everyone will use identical language to describe the same experience and that pilgrims will have to learn to live with differences.

This is expressed particularly powerfully by our Lord in Matthew 5.9: 'Blessed are the peace-makers for they will be called the children of God.' This underlines the point of this psalm. It is not a question simply of being peaceable nor of having that kind of temperament, it is a question of active striving for peace which is characterized by the lack of pride already outlined in the previous Beatitudes. What Jesus is showing is the very life of God himself in action, a life which is a free gift of his Spirit but also has to be struggled for. The fact that peacemakers are called 'children of God' means more than simply being Christian, it means that as they journey to the family home they are positively and actively showing the family likeness because no activity is so Godlike as the creation of *shalom*. Perhaps it is not surprising that it is often at the level of popular piety and devotion that surprising convergences occur. I have often talked with a Roman Catholic friend of how late medieval Catholic songs about the death of Christ recall nothing so much as the 'low church' songs on the same theme. Both use the language of personal adoration, both dwell lovingly on the sufferings of Christ and both are shot through with a very intimate faith which can sometimes be rather embarrassing but at the same time profoundly compelling.

And that is a reminder of the starting point of this chapter which drew attention to the power of music and song. These songs of pilgrimage, represented by Psalms 129—131, have played many tunes and evoked many moods as they have traced the course from the city of destruction to the celestial city. Two further comments will help to focus this more clearly and to glance back at the part of the Lenten pilgrimage already travelled and look forward to its final stages.

First, these are community songs. Although the psalmist has spoken in the first person he has spoken as a representative of the pilgrim community. As already noted, the imagery of the Psalms and the frequent reference to Israel has linked the individual pilgrimage to the larger story of the community. That story is not simply ancient history, a record of what God once did, rather it is a mirror into what God is still doing. Abraham was called to be a pilgrim so that 'all the peoples on earth would be blessed' (Genesis 12.3). Similarly Moses was called to lead the pilgrimage of that community who both in their errors and renewal were to lead to the blessing of the whole world. This forges an indissoluble link between contemporary pilgrims and the whole community of the faithful both in biblical times and across the centuries and traditions. The importance of this in quickening faith and inspiring heroism is difficult to overestimate. We find in Scripture and in spiritual classics continual wells to draw from on the journey through the desert and thus we travel not only with the particular set of people we happen to know but with the pilgrim people across the centuries, 'the great cloud of witnesses' of Hebrews 12.1.

Second, these songs point us forward. While they teach respect and gratitude for the past they warn us not to be enslaved by it. In the next two studies the emphasis will be on how past, present and future are uniquely fused in Christ himself who is not only pilgrim but the goal of pilgrimage. The journey already travelled will help to interpret more faithfully the story of Mary and Jesus while that in turn will give authoritative commentary on the pilgrimage. It will be seen painfully, even brutally, how the journey to Jerusalem leads inevitably to pain, rejection and death, and the call will be heard of someone who himself knows and has experienced the utmost rigours of the pilgrimage journey.

FIVE

How beautiful upon the mountains: Mary travels carrying the Word

Luke 1.39–56

MARY VISITS ELIZABETH

At that time Mary got ready and hurried to a town in the hill country of Judah, where she entered Zechariah's home and greeted Elizabeth. When Elizabeth heard Mary's greeting, the baby leaped in her womb, and Elizabeth was filled with the Holy Spirit. In a loud voice she exclaimed: 'Blessed are you among women, and blessed is the child you will bear! But why am I so favoured, that the mother of my Lord should come to me? As soon as the sound of your greeting reached my ears, the baby in my womb leaped for joy. Blessed is she who has believed that what the Lord has said to her will be accomplished.'

MARY'S SONG

And Mary said:
My soul praises the Lord
   and my spirit rejoices in God my Saviour,
for he has been mindful
   of the humble state of his servant.

From now on all generations will call me
    blessed.
  for the Mighty One has done great things
    for me —
  holy is his name.
His mercy extends to those who fear him,
  from generation to generation.
He has performed mighty deeds with his arm;
  he has scattered those who are proud in
    their inmost thoughts.
He has brought down rulers from their
    thrones
  but has lifted up the humble.
He has filled the hungry with good things
  but has sent the rich away empty.
He has helped his servant Israel,
  remembering to be merciful
to Abraham and his descendants for ever,
  even as he said to our fathers.

Mary stayed with Elizabeth for about three
months and then returned home.

Among the pilgrims of the past, none have caused
more extreme reactions than Mary, mother of
Jesus. Two such reactions are the starting point of
this chapter. One of my favourite tapes is a
haunting collection of tunes called *Glorious Pipes*
played on panpipe and organ by Gheorghe Zamfir
and Diane Bish. In an eloquent introduction to the
music, Gheorghe Zamfir writes a dedication to the
Virgin Mary in these terms:

I wish to have the courage to say that the trace of God may be found in this recording. God at the origin of all things. At the origin of the Holy Trinity which He shares with Jesus and the Virgin Mary, that great mediator for humanity, that the twenty-first century might be different. That is why this music is dedicated to her.

The second reaction is from a sermon I heard many years ago. The sermon was not about Mary. The text was Acts 1 and the preacher, in an offhand way, dismissed verse 14 – 'All these [i.e. the Apostles] with one accord devoted themselves to prayer, together with the women and Mary the mother of Jesus and with his brothers.' 'Mary', he said, 'disappears into the church; she is never heard of again, and that is a woman's place'!

Such views, with greater or lesser sophistication, are commonly expressed and, more fundamentally, often subconsciously held and this makes rational discussion very difficult. I want to suggest that it is useful to begin by examining the reason for such views arising, because when such strong opinions are held there is usually at least some grain of truth in them.

When Protestant hackles rise at the phrase 'Holy Mary, Mother of God', it is helpful to try to find out the origin of the expression. In the early Church, Cyril of Alexandria used the phrase 'Theotokos' – 'Mother of God' – of Mary. He argued this did not mean that 'the nature of the Word or his godhead had its beginning from the holy Virgin, but for as much as his holy Body, endued with a rational soul, was born of her'. Thus the description of Mary had nothing primarily to do with her exalted status but with whether her son could be called 'God'. Yet she was given a unique and awesome privilege: her body carried the living word, her home was the place he grew up in, her love and care were his first earthly experiences. A small detail in Luke 1.35 focuses this in a clear and startling way: 'The angel said to her, ''The Holy Spirit will come upon you, and the power of the Most High will overshadow you.'' ' The word 'overshadow' is used in the Greek Old Testament in Exodus 40.35 of the cloud which symbolized the presence of God resting on the Tent, the portable sanctuary which the Israelites carried on their desert pilgrimage. Thus this young Jewish girl has become the portable sanctuary of the glory of God and to call her 'Holy Mary' is no less than the astonishing truth.

But what is to be made of her as virgin and yet mother. First, I think, we need to reject the idea of 'perpetual virginity'. Mary and Joseph had other children and there is no evidence that these were from a conjectural first marriage of Joseph. What is happening here is something unique and unparalleled and yet not incredible because God the Creator is at work. C. S. Lewis brings this out very powerfully:

> In a normal act of generation the father has no creative function. A microscopic particle of matter from his body, and a microscopic particle from the woman's body, meet ... The human father is merely an instrument, a carrier, often an unwilling carrier, always simply the last in a long line of carriers ... But once, and for a special purpose, God dispensed with that long line which is His instrument: once His life-giving finger touched a woman without passing through the ages of interlocked events.[1]

Lewis is saying that the normal process of procreation has been short-circuited and that God is acting directly rather than through an intermediary. So here Mary is linked with great Old Testament themes of creation and exodus and becomes the centre of Israel and indeed the world's hopes. Thus while Zamfir's words quoted at the beginning of the chapter cannot be taken as they stand they contain the important truth that Mary is a unique individual in an unrepeatable and inimitable role.

But that must be balanced by the complementary truth that Mary is a real woman of flesh and blood, a fellow pilgrim and someone who represents humanity in general and women in particular. The danger of over-emphasizing her uniqueness is that women cannot identify with her, especially when virginity is praised as a higher state than marriage and when the reality of Mary's humanness is underplayed or even denied.

Luke makes it plain that Mary is a representative of a long tradition. Her song, as will be demonstrated, deliberately echoes that earlier Jewish mother Hannah in 1 Samuel 2, and these two women become voices celebrating the life-giving God. Her journey across the Judaean hill country is an echo of the pilgrimages of the returning exiles: 'How beautiful upon the mountains are the feet of him who bring good tidings, who publishes peace, who brings good tidings of good, who publishes salvation, who says to Zion, "Your God reigns" ' (Isaiah 52.7). Mary, in a very literal sense travels the uplands carrying the Word. The Isaiah chapter sees the return from exile as a new exodus, indeed a new creation: 'The Lord has bared his holy arm before the eyes of all the nations; and all the ends of the earth shall see the salvation of our God' (52.10). Mary now repeats that story as she carries the Creator and Redeemer in her womb; Israel is still in exile but a new age has dawned:

> O come, o come Immanuel
> And ransom captive Israel,
> That mourns in lonely exile here . . .

Just as what Mary does echoes the experience of her people in the past so she becomes a model for all future pilgrims. She literally carried the word, all Christian pilgrims do so in a spiritual sense. Her literal journey across the mountains becomes a parable of the journey of faith.

One other question remains. Some may be

wondering why in a book devoted to Lenten pilgrimage a chapter is devoted to what is usually seen as an Advent passage. I think this has an important bearing on the pilgrimage theme. The seasons of the Christian year are important reminders of the great events and realities of our Faith and they need to be learned again as the years pass. Yet Lent, like the other great festivals, is not only a season of the year but a season of the heart. Throughout our pilgrimage we need the realities represented by the festivals of Advent, Christmas, Epiphany, Lent, Easter, Ascension and Pentecost. We do not pass through these seasons and leave them behind as a train passes through stations, we carry all of them with us. Thus in Lent we do not forget that Christ is risen and alive, and in Easter we still need the disciplines of Lent. Indeed we can go further: these are eternal realities about God. This is powerfully expressed in a well-known hymn by Matthew Bridges:

> Crown him the Lord of love;
> behold his hands and side;
> rich wounds, yet visible above,
> In beauty glorified.

The great festivals of the Christian year enshrine truths about God which are fundamental to understanding who he is and what he has done in Christ. Yet in every generation and in every individual they have to be rediscovered and reapplied, and this is where the pilgrimage idea is so fruitful.

This rather long introduction has been necessary in order to come with new eyes to see Mary the mother of our Lord as a fellow pilgrim. Her humanity, her courage, her daring faith, her honesty and realism are at the heart of her pilgrimage. We will look at Mary's burden, for her a very literal one, at Mary's joy, which she shares with Elizabeth, and at Mary's Song, the Magnificat, another of the great songs of pilgrimage.

'Mary got up and hurried into the hill country' says Luke 1.39. There is a sense of urgency in this journey of Mary. It would be some eighty to a hundred miles from Nazareth to this unnamed 'city of Judah'. The human interest in the story is considerable. The angel, by mentioning Elizabeth's pregnancy, had practically suggested that Mary should visit Elizabeth. What Mary needed more than anything else then was some confirmation that this strange experience had been real. Had she imagined the whole thing? She must tell someone. She needed to talk, preferably with another woman. How else could she stand the strain of the nine months waiting?

Mary has already shown her courage in her response to the angel: 'I am the handmaid of the Lord; let it be to me according to your word' (Luke 1.38). Now this is shown further in undertaking this hurried journey. The very literal hazards of bandits, wild animals, primitive caravanserais (like the one she was not allowed into in Chapter 2!) would be very real fears on the journey. Moreover the journey was apparently undertaken alone and we can imagine not a few anxious moments as this young girl fearfully looked at approaching groups of strangers or listened to the sound of approaching footsteps.

But in a way already seen as characteristic of biblical story this journey is full of rich symbolism, especially about pilgrimage. The journey taken by Mary passed over much of the way that Abraham and Sarah would have travelled many centuries before, as well as the countless unnamed pilgrims who sang the 'Psalms of Ascents'. The literal climbing and hazards of the 'hill country' mirror the testing, discipline and dependence on God which is the essence of pilgrimage.

It is also probable that what we are listening to here is part of an autobiography. Fragments of Mary's story in her own words probably lie behind Luke's account. It is an ancient story that Luke met and spoke often with Mary and that much of his material in chapters 1 and 2 of his gospel is based on these conversations. It is fascinating to think of how across the centuries we are in touch with the feelings and emotions behind this wonderful story with its blend of realism and supernaturalism.

There is a reticence and realism about the story which removes it from the realm of fable. This is the story of countless women who throughout the centuries have carried children, often in difficult and dangerous circumstances. The emphasis on her virginity, as already noted, is vital to define her relationship to Jesus, God's son as well as her son. The emphasis on her childbearing, however, shows her as a fellow pilgrim with millions of others.

Moreover, there are many hints throughout the gospels that Mary was not originally a full believer in Christ. This is a fascinating subject in itself but here we will confine ourselves to a number of indications in Luke. At the very end of the nativity and Childhood stories in Chapter 2.48 we read: 'His mother said to him, "Son, why have you treated us like this? Your father and I have been anxiously searching for you?"' Here we are far from the high drama of the Magnificat, this is an anxious parent searching for a lost child and a reminder of Mary's humanity. Similarly in chapter 8.19–21 when Jesus' mother and brothers come to see him we can sense their frustration as they cannot get near him, and their hurt as he says: 'My mother and brothers are those who hear God's word and put it into practice.' In all this we can sense her pilgrimage through the normal human doubts and fears to a deep and lasting faith.

Initially that pilgrimage across the hill country of Judaea led over to the home of Elizabeth and Zechariah. This second phase of the drama could be called Mary's joy, a joy which she shares with Elizabeth. On the human level this is entirely natural: two expectant mothers sharing the joy of child-bearing, both, for very different reasons, in unexpected circumstances.

What is also striking is the deeper significance of this joy. The phrase 'Elizabeth was filled with the Holy Spirit' (v. 41) reminds the reader that the Creator is at work. Just as he is at work in the womb of Mary to plant the word, so the unborn John leaps in response to the unborn Jesus. Similarly in the Song of Songs 2.8 the lover comes 'leaping upon the mountains' and the whole landscape is transformed and renewed by the creating power of love. A further link with Mary's already noted connection with the rich tapestry of allusion and reference is in Elizabeth's question 'why is this granted me, that the mother of my Lord should come to me?' which is reminiscent of 2 Samuel 6.9: 'How can the ark of the Lord come to me?' Mary is indeed the ark of the Covenant carrying the glory of God.

This shared joy is embodied in the word 'blessed', twice used in verse 42. This means much more than 'happy', which is a feeling. It means rather the reality that God is favourably disposed to her whether she feels it or not. She is carrying the Messiah and he is to be blessed as well. We know well, and have not got beyond Luke's stories of the birth and childhood of Jesus before we are reminded, that this will lead to a hard and rocky pilgrimage. This is tersely put by the aged Simeon: 'A sword will pierce your own soul too' (Luke 2.35). Exploring this further will be the subject of the next chapter.

Mary's faith is again emphasized in v. 45: 'Blessed is she who has believed that what the Lord has said to her will be accomplished.' This is yet another indication of how Mary needed the growing faith of a pilgrim, especially when she stood at the foot of the cross with its apparent destruction of all her hopes.

Mary's burden and Mary's joy are the background to her great song of praise usually called the Magnificat.[2] How is Mary going to react to this amazing series of events? Will she rise to the occasion? Will she find suitable words? Will she avoid complacency and pride? Is this an appropriate song for Mary and indeed for her sisters and brothers on pilgrimage? Is it natural that she should use such poetic, archaic language echoing the Old Testament? A commentator on Luke neatly answers this point as follows:

> Anyone who has attended meetings where non-literary people of moderate education engage in extempore prayer, will know that such people generally use language laced with archaic expressions taken from some old translation of the Bible which they have heard read ever since they were children, and mixed with words of hymns written a century or more ago.[3]

I think there is also a deeper point. Luke, characteristically, at this critical point echoes the words of the Old Testament to show that this radically new event is also organically linked to God's ancient purposes. He uses a similar technique in Chapter 24 when the stranger on the Emmaus road speaks of himself and his work in Old Testament terms: 'Beginning with Moses and all the prophets he explained to them what was said in all the Scriptures concerning himself' (24.27). If anyone could have told the story 'in his own words' surely it was Jesus, and, at a more profound level, that is exactly what he did.

We have already explored some of the songs of the ancient pilgrims who travelled to Jerusalem, and now we have another. It is important to keep in mind the various levels of meaning I have already suggested. There is a straightforward meaning: a young Jewish girl expresses her wonder at the miracle of birth. But in this song are all the voices of pilgrims of the past and it reaches out to generations yet unborn. This becomes more obvious when we consider one striking fact. Nowhere in the song does Mary mention that she is to be the mother of the Son of God. So it is that her words can become the marching song of other pilgrims. What then can we learn from Mary about singing the song of pilgrimage?

Mary begins by praising God in language heavily influenced by the Psalms: 'My soul praises the Lord' (v. 47). 'Soul' is a Hebrew way of expressing 'myself' and suggests intense personal involvement. It is vital to see that here she takes her place alongside the rest of sinful humanity: 'My spirit rejoices in God my Saviour.' Like the rest of humankind she stands in need of the grace of God.

When I was a boy I used to get very irritated with the kind of prayer which began something like 'O God who . . .' and which would follow this with various phrases about the nature of God and his mighty acts. 'Why can't they get on with the business of praying?' I would fume. 'God knows who he is and what he has done.' I can still understand this irritation but it did miss an important point. What I thought of as unnecessary padding is, in fact, 'the business of praying'. Only because of who God is and what he has done can we pray at all. Praying is about relationship. God knows, of course. But we do not always know or take seriously what kind of God it is we are praying to. That does not mean that every prayer must begin with an outline of the attributes of the Trinity and a recitation of biblical history, but that all prayer must begin with an awareness of the overwhelming greatness of God.

Mary goes on (vv. 48–49) to apply this to her own situation. She succeeds in doing this without being self-important and self-centred. This is a recurring problem in speaking of our faith. If we are not personal we are in danger of seeing God as remote and aloof. If we tell anecdotes about ourselves we are in danger of usurping the centre of the stage. This problem is acute in Christian testimonies and autobiographies. How does Mary avoid this pitfall?

I think she does it by the way she looks at the whole astonishing drama in which she has been caught up. This is a unique moment, yet in another sense it is simply a special example of what God always does. The echoes of Hannah's glad song as she held the baby Samuel remind us that she is simply one more Jewish girl whom God has blessed. Moreover, all future generations will be able to celebrate the mercy of this same God. Her thoughts soar as she contemplates the power of this God whose purposes cannot be thwarted.

This leads on very naturally for her to sing of the mighty acts of God. It is important to realize that Mary is not simply talking in general terms of the power of God but especially focusing on the Exodus which is seen throughout the Old Testament as the historical example of God's 'mighty acts'. That event itself was the demonstration in time and space of God's power as Creator. With trembling excitement Mary realizes that their God is intervening again. Their nation is a conquered province, there is no king, Jerusalem is not a free city but Yahweh is on the move and calling his people again to the pilgrim adventure. Something of that excitement is felt in Narnia when Mr Beaver whispers to the children: 'They say Aslan is on the move – perhaps has already landed.'[4]

Luke picks up this theme in another climactic moment. In his account of the event called the transfiguration, Moses and Elijah speak of 'his ''exodus'' which he was to accomplish at Jerusalem' (9.31). Jesus is to lead his people across the desert to the promised land and his dying and rising is the guarantee that the goal will be reached. The pilgrimage theme is bound up in Luke's presentation of Jesus and this will be more fully explored in the next chapter.

But it is just here that doubts and questions begin to arise. Granted that praise begins with the greatness of God and the celebration of his mighty acts, how does that work out in the 'real' world? Can we really believe that the mundane events of our lives, the grey days of the routine grind are part of God's loving purposes? Are we in fact on a pilgrimage at all? Do we just have the illusion of movement as when we are waiting for our train to leave and the one on the next track does and for a few seconds we think we are on our way?

It is this kind of question the next part of the song addresses. Verses 51–53 show that God's actions are not mere occasional hit and run raids. Rather, they bring about a permanent revolution. This is a radical revolution which goes right to the core of basic attitudes: 'he has scattered those who are proud in their inmost thoughts.' In other words it is not 'the kind of revolution which simply replaces one set of top people with another'.[5] Rather what is envisaged is a community built on the meeting of real needs and the abolition of artificial distinctions.

I think this will help us to avoid two opposite misunderstandings of this part of the Magnificat. One is to interpret it exclusively in social and political terms and ignore the emphasis on inner attitudes and knowledge of God. This too readily casts the cloak of sanctity over regimes which replace corrupt and evil power structures. All too many revolutions begin in idealism and end in another tyranny. Our own century has seen many examples of that. The old Tsarist regime in Russia needed to be replaced and few mourned its passing. Now some years after the fall of the Berlin Wall we can see how Stalinism simply was another set of oppressors. Nor can we be complacent. The continuing turmoil in Russia as well as, at the time of writing, renewed horrors in Bosnia, remind us that mere politics will not introduce the Kingdom of God.

However, we must avoid the other error of simply spiritualizing the language of verses 51–53 as in the hymn by C. G. Alexander:

> The rich man in his castle,
> The poor man at his gate.
> God made them high or lowly,
> And ordered their estate.

This attitude simply refuses to accept the radical call to discipleship and pilgrimage and asks us to baptize the establishment in the hope of better things in the world to come. This attitude complacently accepts cardboard city, mass unemployment, poor housing and unscrupulous landlords.

Both attitudes must balance the other. Unjust structures, institutionalized greed and the corrupting love of materialism must be challenged and changed by every peaceful means. The environment must be cherished and protected. Society must be fair and just. But these on their own will fail without that radical transformation of human hearts which is a result of the personal response of faith to the grace of God in Christ. Without this hearts will still break, relationships still be poisoned, society still be eaten up with selfishness.

The trouble with this is that it is easy for us to agree in general terms, but a little voice in us says: 'My nature will never change, my weaknesses can never be overcome. All this talk about love and sharing is fine but you don't know the people I live with, you don't understand the kind of colleagues I have to work with, the pressures on me are something else.' That feeling is real and I think that is where verses 54 and 55 are so important. 'He has helped his servant Israel, remembering to be merciful to Abraham . . .' That immediately focuses on the specific and the particular. The names 'Israel' and 'Abraham' remind us of these stories in the book of Genesis where the doings of Mary's ancestors are recounted. In our look at Abraham we already identified those very personal weaknesses which revealed a God who can and does work through them. Abraham became a great pilgrim not because he was perfect but because he dared everything and laid himself totally open to God's leading.

But this is not confined to Abraham, it extends 'to his descendants for ever, even as he said to our fathers'. Just as old words and phrases are reshaped creatively so lives are inspired by the same spirit and new pilgrims start the journey.

All this, I think, is crystallized in the words 'mercy' and 'merciful'. The Magnificat has, as we have seen, a robust concern for justice. Justice, though, on its own is not enough. Justice will bring down oppressive rulers and feed the hungry. What justice on its own cannot do is to ensure that oppressive regimes are replaced by just ones or that the hungry when fed will necessarily care for others who are still hungry. Justice, in fact, is creating the conditions where a more dynamic and life-giving force – what is here called 'mercy' – is able to work. A couple of Old Testament references will help to make this clear. Psalm 103.11 says: 'For as high as the heavens are above the earth so great is his mercy for those who fear him.' In other words, God's mercy takes us into a different dimension. And again, in the same psalm, mercy has an eternal quality: 'from everlasting to everlasting, the Lord's mercy is with those who fear him.' Also, throughout the New Testament, mercy is particularly associated with the love God has shown us in Christ. One example will do: 'God who is rich in mercy made us alive with Christ.' It is mercy which creates the life of God in us.

An example from everyday life will illustrate this. A woman is raped and her attacker is caught and imprisoned. That is justice. But justice will not heal her shattered confidence, brutal invasion of her privacy and all the trauma of her terrifying experience. She needs to be loved and accepted unconditionally, surrounded by the caring concern that will help her on the climb back to normality. Only mercy and not mere justice can do that. Similarly her attacker is justly imprisoned and serves his sentence. But that on its own will not prevent what caused the offence in the first place. Once again mercy, not sloppy and sentimental but firmly forcing him to look into his own darkness, confront the evil and ask for help, will be the road to recovery.

Mercy is a powerful and life-changing force sweeping through society with tremendous power. It belongs in the places where caring and dedicated people look after the incontinent elderly; where Samaritans spend time with the lonely and desperate teenager; where the unwashed and unloved children of Calcutta are cared for by Mother Theresa. And it springs especially from the sense of being forgiven and accepted. If accepted by God, then we can accept others and truly love them.

Corrie ten Boom, the courageous Dutch Christian, who with her sister was interned in Ravensbrück concentration camp, tells of a moving incident some time after the Second World War was over. Her sister, Bessie, had in fact died in the camp. Corrie was speaking at a meeting and recounting her experiences during that awful time. As she spoke she was aware of a man who seemed vaguely familiar who was looking at her somewhat oddly. At the end of the meeting as she shook hands with people this man approached her. In a flash of recognition she recognized who he was. He was one of the guards in the notorious camp. She thought of Bessie's wasted body and felt she would never shake hands with this man,

Christian though he had now become. She prayed desperately, and reluctantly held out her hand. As she did so she felt a sudden surge of warmth in her arm and found herself filled with a love not her own and was able to greet him. That was not mere justice, it was mercy.

Two others matters will bring this chapter to an end. By any standard, the Magnificat is a wonderful song of pilgrimage full of a life-changing and mould-breaking faith. Yet it is not all high excitement for Mary. As the song dies away, we read: 'Mary stayed with Elizabeth for about three months and then returned home' (v. 56). These eternal truths about God's love and justice are now to be lived out in the mundane realities of everyday living. Soon there will be another journey and the promised birth in circumstances which seem to mock the exalted language of the promise. Pilgrimage involves the routine grind: the Monday mornings, washing the dishes, visiting relatives and the other thousand and one tasks and experiences which make up our lives. Yet all has been transformed. These routines will never have the same predictability again. The Creator Spirit is on the move and literally anything can happen.

The other thought is this. Mary's uniqueness and yet naturalness links her both with our everyday lives and the startling possibilities that beckon us. For us too these possibilities are beyond our imagining and yet the natural outcome of our background and circumstances. That is what it means to be uniquely loved:

Tell out, my soul, the glories of his word!
Firm is his promise and his mercy sure:
Tell out, my soul, the greatness of the Lord
to children's children and for evermore.

(Timothy Dudley-Smith)

SIX

Who would true valour see?:
Jesus the author and finisher
of our faith

Luke 9.51

As the time approached for him to be taken up to heaven, Jesus resolutely set out for Jerusalem.

Hebrews 12.1–3

Therefore, since we are surrounded by such a great cloud of witnesses, let us throw off everything that hinders and the sin that so easily entangles, and let us run with perseverance the race marked out for us. Let us fix our eyes on Jesus, the author and perfecter of our faith, who for the joy set before him endured the cross, scorning its shame, and sat down at the right hand of the throne of God. Consider him who endured such opposition from sinful men, so that you will not grow weary and lose heart.

Some haunting words from T. S. Eliot will serve to introduce our last meditation on pilgrimage.

> We shall not cease from exploration
> And the end of all our exploring

> Will be to arrive where we started
> And know the place for the first time.[1]

Few have captured more memorably the sense of the passing of time, the continuity and yet newness, the mingled anticipation and fear of 'travelling hopefully' than Eliot. This chapter will try to explore this theme more fully by focusing on Jesus himself, both as pilgrim who walked the way before us and now walks with us, and as the goal of our pilgrimage.

The particular passages which illuminate this are Luke 9 and Hebrews 12. Luke 9.51 is the turning point of that gospel: 'As the time approached for him to be taken up to heaven, Jesus resolutely set out for Jerusalem.' From that point until chapter 19.27 Luke gives a lengthy account of Jesus' journey from Galilee to Jerusalem, and these chapters continually emphasize the idea of journey.[2] But when we study Luke's material more closely we begin to see what he is suggesting. It is not mere geography, because Jesus does not take a direct route from Galilee to Jerusalem and when he eventually approaches the city, he does so from the south, from Jericho. It is, in the fullest possible sense, a pilgrimage. Like his ancestors, such as those who sang the ascent psalms, he is travelling to Jerusalem to celebrate the great Passover festival which marked the creation of the nation. Yet poignantly he is himself to be the sacrificial lamb and his death to be life for the world. And so much of Luke's material in these chapters is relevant to this: the sending out of the seventy-two disciples (17.1–12); the life of the kingdom in the parables of the Good Samaritan (10.25–37), the Prodigal Son (15.11–32) and the terrifying story of the Rich Man and Lazarus (16.19–31).

The real key to understanding what Luke is saying here is in the words of 9.51: 'for him to be taken up to heaven'. This is the real goal of pilgrimage. Jerusalem is, of course, no nearer heaven than is Galilee, but, as we have seen, it is a symbol of the city of God and becomes both part of the journey and an anticipation of the destination. There is a wonderful passage at the end of the Narnia stories which captures this sense of longing and searching aroused in us by places we love, and which C. S. Lewis regarded as evidence of our longing for heaven:

> The new one [i.e. Narnia] was a deeper country: every rock and flower and blade of grass looked as if it meant more. I can't describe it any better than that: if you ever get there you will know what I mean.
>
> It was the Unicorn who summed up what everyone was feeling. He stamped his right fore-hoof on the ground and neighed and then cried:
>
> 'I have come home at last! This is my real country! I belong here. This is the land I have been looking for all my life, though I never knew it till now. The reason why we loved

the old Narnia is that it sometimes looked a
little like this.'[3]

This links the pilgrimage of Jesus with all those
other pilgrims of past, present and future and
shows that 'travelling hopefully' is already part of
the goal.

Similarly, Hebrews 12 speaks of Jesus who not
only ran the race but now is 'at the right hand of
the throne of God'. The context of this passage is
important for it gathers history and symbol of
biblical pilgrimage and uses these in a new and
creative way. In Chapter 11 the whole of biblical
and later Church history is seen as a pilgrimage of
faith, and we have already noticed how this is
shown in the stories of Abraham and Moses. Later
in Chapter 12 the writer describes the goal of
pilgrimage:

> But you have come to Mount Zion, to the
> heavenly Jerusalem, the city of the living
> God. You have come to the thousands upon
> thousands of angels in joyful assembly, to the
> church of the firstborn, whose names are
> written in heaven. You have come to God,
> the judge of all, to the spirits of righteous
> people made perfect, to Jesus the mediator of
> a new covenant.

There we have it. The ancient pilgrimage to the
literal Zion is part of the life of eternity and thus
the goal is no anticlimax but a fulfilment of our
deepest longings. Thus the author focuses on the

death and triumph of Christ in which there is a unique blend of past, present and future. It is these three areas we shall examine, using the passages in Luke and Hebrews.

People tend to have extreme views on the past. Some of us idealize it, romanticize it and even try to live in it. Others despise it, ignore it and think there is nothing to learn from it. Pilgrimage requires from us a more dynamic attitude to the past and we shall now explore, with the help of our two passages, how the past, both historical and personal, can inspire pilgrims in the present.

The background of Jesus setting out on the last stage of his pilgrimage to Jerusalem is that great story of the event we call the transfiguration (Luke 9.28–36). Here the two great representatives of 'the Law and the Prophets' appear in glory with Jesus. This means, in the first place, that our pilgrimage through the Old Testament is most necessary in order to understand Jesus. We cannot genuinely be pilgrims in his footsteps unless we drink deeply from the wells of the Jewish Scriptures as he did. This will link our own personal stories with the great story of God leading his people. Otherwise we shall be like the man who delivered a tirade against the Old Testament, taking as his text the words of Jesus in Matthew 22.40 which in the King James version read: 'On these two command-ments hang all the law and the prophets.' Unfortunately, he chose to base his remarks only on the last phrase and with great passion urged his hearers to 'hang all the Law and the Prophets'.

The sheer richness of this story is breathtaking. For a few heart-stopping moments the goal of pilgrimage has become a reality on the journey. The 'not yet' has invaded the 'now'. The destination of the pilgrim is seen not merely as something in the far future but as already existing and all around us. While this is a real incident on an actual mountain, this is also the sacred mountain the place of prayer and vision. More than that, this is the new exodus, because in verse 31 Luke makes that startlingly plain: 'They spoke about his departure, which he was about to bring to fulfilment at Jerusalem.' The word translated 'departure' is 'exodus' and links Jesus' death and resurrection with God's rescue of his people and their pilgrimage across the desert to the promised land. Few things will inspire us more than this realization that we are part of this great pilgrimage of the faithful throughout the ages.

And yet it is precisely at this point that we can be side-tracked and the past become a place to settle rather than a well to drink from so that we may pursue our journey renewed and refreshed. This is exactly what Peter wants to do: ' "Master, it is good for us to be here. Let us put up three shelters – one for you, one for Moses and one for Elijah." (He did not know what he was saying).' But neither Peter, nor we, can remain meditating on one experience, however glorious. There is work to be done: at the foot of the mountain there is a distressed father with his demented son who needs healing. There is the road to travel to the cross.

God is continually moving us on and teaching us both to respect the past and refuse to be bound by it. This is further underlined in Hebrews 12. The great gallery of the faithful, famous and nameless, which is Hebrews 11 is a glorious panorama of the pilgrimage of the faithful which merges in Chapter 12 into a rousing call to daring faith and adventurous pilgrimage in our own day. History must lead to action and to 'running with perseverance the race set before us' (v. 1). This is particularly focused in the phrase in verse 2: 'Let us fix our eyes on Jesus.' The translation 'let us fix our eyes' is a paraphrase of a word which occurs nowhere else in the New Testament.[4] More literally it means 'looking away from towards Jesus'. The obvious question is 'looking away from whom or what?'

Some commentators argue that the expressions in verse 1 – 'everything that hinders and the sin that so easily entangles' are what we are to 'look away from towards'. 'Everything that hinders' is literally everything which prevents us effectively following the life of a pilgrim. It could be money, ambition, our homes, relationships which become obsessive, hobbies which take up inordinate amounts of time or excessive caution. Notice that none of these things are wrong in themselves, they are part of normal, healthy living. However, any of them can become a snare and delusion. 'The sin that so easily entangles' is not, I think, sinfulness in general, so much as the particular besetting sin which is different for each of us. This is probably why the author does not specify the sin. If a particular one were named, the temptation would be to think either 'that's not my besetting sin, so I can safely ignore this', or 'that is my besetting sin, I must be much worse than other people'. Undoubtedly to look away from both the good things taken to excess and the besetting sins is right, but it seems hardly worth saying because it is obvious and rather trite.

What I want to suggest is that the writer is urging us to look away from the 'great cloud of witnesses' themselves.[5] Be inspired by them, honour them but do not be obsessed by them. There is only one pilgrim to look to for he is Lord of past, present and future.

Why is it necessary to give this warning of the wrong use of the past? I think this can be illustrated by contrasting the museums of my youth with modern museums. When I was a schoolboy, a trip to a museum was greeted with a groan. Museums then were venerable institutions where relics of the past were preserved behind glass, remote and untouchable. An air of closeness and lifelessness hung over them and it was difficult to imagine people of the past as living, breathing human beings. What a contrast with museums now. Go to the Yorvik centre in York and travel back down the centuries in time cars to the sights, sounds and even the smells of medieval York. Go to the ABC museum in the same city and participate in exciting reconstructions of the material remains of the city's life. Have a similar experience in Oxford in the Oxford Story or visit the wonderful evocation of late medieval England in the Warwick the Kingmaker exhibition at Warwick Castle. Readers will no doubt know many other places, I simply mention a few with which I am familiar. What these museums do is show us our organic link with the past and bring the people and events to life. They are a wonderful blend of the timelessness of human experience and the ancient expressed in contemporary ways.

Now that is what a pilgrim faith means. When we dwell in the past we are trying to preserve it under glass, and we are imitating mannerisms and canonizing incidental and temporary ways of expressing the faith.

The village on the east coast of Scotland where I grew up used to be nicknamed 'the holy city', not so much because of the sanctity of its inhabitants as because of the remarkable number and variety of places of worship. As well as the Church of Scotland, there was a Congregational Church, three varieties of the Brethren, the Salvation Army and a somewhat elusive group called 'The Pilgrims'; all these for a community of less than two thousand people. Much of this reflected a religious awakening in the early years of the century when a fisherman turned evangelist named Jock Troup had preached in the various fishing ports on the east coast from Peterhead to Yarmouth. Many of my grandfather's generation, who like him were involved in fishing, had been caught up in this revival fervour and this led to the establishment of flourishing Christian communities. Naturally these reflected the lifestyle and idioms of their time. Sadly, as time passed and the early fervour died what remained was a kind of museum-like faith, preserving under glass the forms and customs of a bygone age. Many of these once-flourishing groups have gone, their premises now private houses. In others, a few elderly people keep the doors open but the life and the glory has gone. This is not, of course, to question the sincerity of their motives but to point out that the way to keep faith is not to shut it away, but to live it, preach it and demonstrate its relevance to every new generation. The only way to be pilgrims is to draw from the past but live in the present.

And that brings us neatly to our second main area which is the present and how the reality of Christ's pilgrimage can help us now. In the Luke 9 passage, Peter thought the kingdom had already come. In a sense he was right. The life of the world to come had broken into this world. A glimpse of the kingdom had shown it was already there, and on the way to the cross this was a tremendous boost to faith. Thus the experience on the mountain of transfiguration is a 'trailer' of the glory to follow. But that glory must await the future for its full revelation. The pilgrim way, the way of the cross, is for the present. Jesus makes this plain in Luke 9.23: 'If anyone would come after me, he must deny himself and take up his cross daily and follow me.' That word 'daily' is vital. Pilgrimage is not merely a matter of the spectacular dash but of the regular routines and disciplines. Yet the transfiguration story also reminds us of the power and nearness of the other world, and I think this has two implications.

The first is that we can expect to have glimpses of glory from time to time. This is true both of churches and individuals. We can expect growth, healing, peace and every other kind of blessing. There are these golden times when worship seems to be heightened, when Bible reading is a joy and when prayer is eagerly anticipated. The moments which sometimes make it easy to imagine that the kingdom has already stolen upon us.

The second is the mirror image of that. Because the kingdom has not yet come we can also expect reversals and bitter disappointments. We can expect hostility, decline and apathy. We still sin and we still die. It is exciting to read of churches coming alive, moribund structures being revitalized, surging crowds and bright singing. But we know that just as often we hear of dead churches, premises now garages or flats, and sometimes these are the same churches.

How are we to hold these two in tension and to avoid either triumphalism or despair? The first thing to realize is that both situations are realities and if we are enjoying the first not to imagine complacently that it will always be like that. Nor if we are enduring the second should we despairingly believe that nothing can change it. Read the great classics of spiritual pilgrimage and find how often the mountain of vision and the valley of dry bones lie close together. Neither are ends in themselves, they are part of our journey to the goal. Kipling's words are helpful here:

> If you can meet with Triumph and Disaster,
> And treat these two imposters just the same.
>
> (from 'If')

The word 'imposters' is very important. It does not mean that the circumstances are unreal. Rather the truth is that they are passing circumstances which can become 'means of grace' to us. This will help us to be grateful and humble in times of triumph and to, as the old hymn says, 'trust and obey' in times of darkness.

But further, both the Luke and Hebrews passages speak of a life of discipline and discipleship as we follow Jesus daily. Both place discipleship firmly in the context of the way of the cross. This reminds us in the first place that Jesus by his death and resurrection does not only provide the supreme example of a pilgrim but by his sacrifice and victory gives us the power to be pilgrims at all. Indeed, as Paul says in Galatians 2.20: 'I have been crucified with Christ and I no longer live but Christ lives in me.' This means in the second place, that to 'imitate' Jesus is not simply like imitating Moses and Elijah. After all, as we have seen, this can easily become a rather mechanical following of external patterns. 'Crucifying the flesh' and 'denying ourselves' and our indulgences is, of course, an important part of Christian pilgrimage, but that can easily become a subtle form of pride. What is being spoken of here is an opening of our lives to the power of the crucified and risen Lord. Allowing ourselves to be the recipients of God's grace is what makes the imitation of Christ possible. The fact that Jesus has ascended and is 'at the right hand of the throne of God' is the guarantee that all the other pilgrims will arrive.

This brings us to the third main area, which is pilgrimage into the future. The two phrases — 'Taken up into heaven' (Luke 9.51) and 'sat down at the right hand of God' (Hebrews 12.2) introduce that idea. 'Travelling hopefully' has now become 'arrival' and the reality of the goal sheds significant light on pilgrimage here and now. 'Sat down' does not imply doing nothing but rather shows the abiding significance of Christ's death and resurrection. It is at this point we can pause and see how our writers bring together many of the themes we have explored and also make some final comments on how this enables us to journey with confidence into the future.

The first thing to emphasize is that Jesus himself is at the centre of all true pilgrimage. This is particularly vividly shown in the transfiguration story in Luke 9. Moses and Elijah have not the same status, they are simply fellow pilgrims, great and inspiring indeed but not the goal of the journey. Thus we must listen to the voice from the heavenly glory and fix our eyes on Jesus. There is a fascinating detail in the story which illustrates who Jesus is and how unnecessary it was to linger on the holy mountain. Peter said: 'Master, it is good for us to be here. Let us put up three shelters – one for you, one for Moses and one for Elijah.' The word 'shelter' is the word used for 'tent' or 'tabernacle' with all its associations of God's presence travelling with the community through the desert. The cloud which 'enveloped' them is the same glory which, as we saw in the previous chapter, 'overshadowed' Mary and caused her to bear the Word.

It is Jesus himself who is the 'tent' of glory. Two further references will make this clear. John 1.14 says: 'The Word became flesh and lived for a while among us.' 'Lived' can literally be translated 'pitched his tent', and that God's presence in the desert is referred to is made plain by the next phrase 'we have seen his glory'. The 'glory' of God was especially associated with the Tent in the desert. When that Tent was first set up: 'The cloud covered the Tent of meeting and the glory of the Lord filled the tabernacle' (Exodus 40.34). So the reality of the experience of God on the desert wanderings is nothing less than the presence of the Lord Christ himself. But not only is that associated with 'travelling hopefully', it is one of the metaphors used to describe the 'arrival'. Thus we read in Revelation 21.3: 'And I heard a loud voice from the throne saying, ''Now the dwelling of God is with men, and he will live with them. They will be his people and God himself will be with them and be their God.'' ' Again 'dwelling' would be more accurately translated 'tent' or 'tabernacle' and this is the reality to which all the symbols of the tabernacle point.

The fact that Jesus has reached the goal 'at the right hand of God' is the guarantee that all other pilgrims will safely arrive as well. Indeed the Hebrews passage makes the point that many have arrived already. 'We are surrounded by a great cloud of witnesses' (Hebrews 12.1). This does not merely imply a crowd of passive spectators watching from the grandstand, rather active pilgrims who had proved and testified to their faith.

None of this means that pilgrims are those who are 'too heavenly-minded to be of any earthly use'. I wonder how many readers have ever met anyone like that. I most certainly have not. What it does mean is that the present pilgrimage is seen in its total perspective which involves taking the arrival seriously. Indeed the more firmly we believe that one day Christ will wind up the affairs of this world and introduce a better one, the more urgently we will engage in all lawful and worthy activities 'until he comes'.

And that faces us again with the practicalities and possibilities of pilgrimage. Throughout this book we have seen the vital importance of bringing the eternal and the contemporary together. The whole context of the Hebrews 12 passage is how faith in the unseen God has enormous consequences both in the everyday world and in the whole sweep of history. Thus Hebrews 11 memorably focuses on the great climactic moments of the pilgrimages of Abraham and Moses as well as sweeping through great tracts of sacred history. Hebrews 13 continues the pilgrimage theme in such practical matters as 'entertaining strangers', marriage relationships and the right use of money.

We have already noticed how Luke 9 begins a long section in the gospel where the idea of journey and pilgrimage is emphasized. One particular incident will focus clearly many of the issues which have been raised throughout this book. This is the story in Luke 18.18–30 usually called 'The Rich Young Ruler', where a prominent and wealthy individual expresses a desire to become a pilgrim. Jesus speaks to him in some very penetrating and challenging words: 'You will lack one thing. Sell everything you have and give to the poor, and you will have treasure in heaven. Then come follow me' (Luke 18.22). In this story Jesus is forcing that man and all of us to a radical reconsideration of our priorities. What is life about? What at heart do we think as most important? A girl who had just completed her A-levels successfully was speaking to her vicar. He asked her what she intended to do. 'I'm going to University to study law', she replied. 'And after, that?' he asked. 'I'll be apprenticed to a legal firm and if I do well who knows, I may even become a QC, perhaps even a judge, with greater opportunities for women, nowadays', she said. 'And after that?' said the vicar. 'Well, I hope to have married and have children', the girl said.

'And after that?' he asked. By now the girl was a little exasperated; 'Why do you keep on saying, "and after that?"' 'Why set your ambitions so low?' replied the vicar, 'Why not consider Eternity?' It is with just such a question that this story confronts us. Because here in this incident we are faced starkly with what pilgrimage means.

But what do these words of Jesus mean? Is 'selling all we have' a universal command and unless we obey it can we truly be said to be pilgrims at all? I think it is helpful to see that Jesus in fact is saying two things: one is 'sell all you have', the second is 'follow me', and both of these are governed by the phrase 'you still lack one thing'; or in the vivid words of older versions 'one thing is needful'.

So let us try to grapple with this hard saying of Jesus. I think there are two dangers in interpreting 'Sell everything you have and give to the poor'. The first is to water it down to suit a comfortable, complacent Western lifestyle. 'What Jesus *really* meant is that we ought to give more to Christian Aid, Tear Fund and Amnesty International. We ought to put five pounds instead of one pound into the collection plate.' Undoubtedly these kind of comments are true, but the problem is that we could probably do all or many of these things without our discipleship becoming in any way more committed or our lifestyle affected in any profound way.

The second is to interpret the words with a mechanical literalism as an absolute command for every Christian everywhere. Some have indeed taken this command literally, most famously St Francis of Assisi, and, in our own day, Mother Theresa. But what about the Christian family struggling on income support with a father who is long-term unemployed? What about the single parent in the tower-block struggling to bring up children on a pittance? What about, less obviously, the middle-class family, comfortably off on paper, but who have already given sacrificially and have no material security for the future? What does this text say to such people?

I suggest that Jesus is saying that in all of us there is a basic hindrance to discipleship. In the case of the rich young ruler it was his great wealth. He would continue to trust in this and never really trust the Lord. With others it might well be different. With some it could be career, glittering achievements and reputation. With others it could be intellect, it could be ambition, it could even be the church as an institution replacing a personal relationship with Christ. It could be anything at all, and each of us knows what it is in our lives. That is the negative side, the 'one thing needful' for us to deal with before true pilgrimage can begin.

But now to the second statement; the simple words 'follow me'. This is the common element throughout the gospels whoever Jesus is calling. The basic hindrance to discipleship, the one thing that needs to be removed is different for all of us, and what is more, different for each of us at particular times in our lives. But for everyone at all times, the call to follow, to be a disciple, to be a pilgrim is also the 'one thing needful'.

Throughout this book we have explored in different ways what following Christ means. We have seen the importance of drawing from the deep wells of the Bible and also the spiritual classics. We have reflected on the importance of prayer and worship and on fellowship with pilgrims of the past as well as the present. We have seen how the theme of pilgrimage links Christians across the centuries and the traditions because Christ is the way and the end. Whatever our circumstances, temperaments or traditions, the 'one thing needful' is the radical call to discipleship and following Christ. If you live out your life in obscurity known only to your family and friends, one thing is needful, that you follow Christ. If you rise to heights of great eminence and your name becomes a household word; one thing is needful, that you follow Christ. If you struggle to make ends meet and never know how you are going to pay your next bill; one thing is needful, that you follow Christ. If you have lots of money, a nice home and a secure job; one thing is needful, that you follow Christ. If your life is one crisis and disaster after another; one thing is needful, that you follow Christ. And if, improbably, you go through life with no real disappointment or heartbreak; then one thing is needful, that you follow Christ.

Notes

1 Looking for a city: going on pilgrimage

1 R. L. Stevenson: 'El Dorado' vi.

2 C. S. Lewis puts this wonderfully: 'All their life in the world and all their adventures in Narnia had only been the cover and title page: now at last they were beginning Chapter One of the Great Story which no one on earth has read: which is forever: in which every chapter is better than the one before.' *The Last Battle* (Bodley Head, 1956), p. 172.

3 *The Way of a Pilgrim*, translated from the Russian by R. M. French (SPCK, 1974).

4 Shirley Du Boulay, *The Road to Canterbury – A Modern Pilgrimage* (HarperCollins, 1994).

5 Augustine describes this in the *Confessions*, Bk 8, Ch. 12: 'I was . . . weeping all the while with the most bitter sorrow in my heart when all at once I heard the sing-song voice of a child in a nearby house. Whether it was the voice of a boy or girl I cannot say, but again and again it repeated the refrain, "Take it and read, take it and read" . . . this could only be a divine command to open my book of Scripture and read the first passage on which my eyes should fall . . . [I read] "Not in revelling and drunkenness, not in lust and wantonness, not in quarrels and rivalries. Rather arm yourself with the Lord Jesus Christ."'

6 The word translated 'walking' suggests a continuous strolling and has the idea of regular activity.

3 Guide me, O Thou Great Redeemer: the community's uncertain faith

1 A similar issue can be seen in the so-called 'Plague Stories' in Exodus 7–11. Ten times we read 'The Lord hardened Pharaoh's heart' and ten times that 'Pharaoh hardened his heart'. The implication again is of a deliberate balance between God's sovereignty and human responsibility.

2 The NIV translation does not bring out clearly the connection between the verses. Verse 8 reads better as in the RSV: '*Then* came the Amalekites . . .', with the *then* emphasizing the connection.

3 There are still many problems relating to the literal fighting and killing in the Old Testament but these are not especially relevant to this study. What I am emphasizing is that we cannot simply read off from the surface of the text literal applications.

4 A good example of this is John Buchan who writes: 'I never consciously invented with a pen in my hand; I waited until the story had told itself and then wrote it down.' *Memory Hold-The-Door* (Hodder and Stoughton, 1940), p. 195.

5 See N. O'Donoghue, *The Holy Mountain* (Dominican Publications, 1983).

4 The steep ascent: the community's songs of pilgrimage

1 The point is made by A. Moyer in the *New Bible Commentary* (3rd edn, IVP, 1970), p. 529.

2 See John Goldingay, *Praying the Psalms* (Grove

Spirituality Booklet No. 44) for a useful discussion
of this issue.

5 How beautiful upon the mountains: Mary travels carrying the Word

1 C. S. Lewis, *Miracles* (Fontana, 1963), p. 142.
2 Some argue that the song was in fact uttered by
Elizabeth, and others that it was inserted into
Luke's original text. If my argument in this chapter
is valid, then it can be seen that it is a natural
culmination of Mary's experience and feelings. That
does not mean it was not reworked and polished
later.
3 D. W. Gooding, *According to Luke: A new exposition of
the Third Gospel* (IVP, 1987), p. 42.
4 C. S. Lewis, *The Lion, the Witch and the Wardrobe*
(Lions, 1992), p. 65.
5 N. D. O'Donoghue, *The Holy Mountain* (Dominican
Publications, 1983), p. 12.

6 Who would true valour see?: Jesus the author and finisher of our faith

1 T. S. Eliot, 'Little Gidding' V, *The Four Quartets*
(Faber and Faber, 1994).
2 By contrast, Mark's account of the journey is
confined to 9.30–10.52, and Matthew's to chapters
19 and 20. John does not mention this journey.
3 C. S. Lewis, *The Last Battle* (Lions, 1992), pp. 160–
161.
4 The word has the nuance of 'looking away from the
immediate surroundings'.

5 This suggestion, as far as I can discover, is only made in an old but useful book on Hebrews 11: *The Triumph of Faith* by G. Campbell Morgan (Pickering and Inglis, no date given, but presumably Second World War because it is printed on 'war economy standard' paper), pp. 116–117.